The 50th Birthda
Book

Fun Facts, Quizzes & Memory-Lane Challenges For 50-Year-Olds (50th Birthday Gift)

B N William

BNW William

Your Cheat Sheet (No Peeking at the Answers)

Before you dive in, here's a little gift: scan the QR code and join our FREE weekly newsletter.

Every week you'll get fresh quizzes, mind-bending facts, and hilarious history stories delivered straight to your inbox. It's like keeping the fun of this book going, long after you've closed the cover.

We'll even send you an exclusive peek at our Amazon #1 Bestseller, Shut the Fact Up.

No spam, no boring stuff. Just facts that surprise, delight, and occasionally make you laugh out loud.
Scan the QR code and start your weekly trivia fix today!

Opening Salvo

Welcome to the *50th Quiz Book*, where history lectures are replaced by pub banter, and trivia means more than just remembering who won Eurovision in 1974 (though that might pop up). Inside, you'll stumble across Vietnam timelines next to Beatles rooftop gigs, presidents with pet alligators, and sports moments that made jaws drop harder than Zidane's infamous headbutt. You'll see disasters collide with disco, capitals that refuse to stay put, and cocktails that carry passports from the wrong countries.

Expect pop culture to elbow history in the ribs, food myths to rub shoulders with politics, and TV finales to sit right next to Cold War standoffs. The rules are simple: read, laugh, and try not to flip to the answers too quickly. Whether you're a quiz master's in training or just here for the weird facts, buckle up. This book doesn't test memory. It tests curiosity.

Round 1 – Quotable Quest

Words outlive their speakers. Some lines become battle cries, other punchlines, and a few just refuse to leave pop culture's echo chamber. This round is all about those unforgettable phrases that shaped how we talk, argue, laugh, and even order popcorn at the movies.

Q1. Complete the Famous Quote

Fill in the missing word(s):

1. "In space, no one can hear you ____."
2. "Elementary, my dear ____."
3. "Life is like a box of ____."
4. "May the ____ be with you."
5. "Here's looking at you, ____."

Q2. "I'm gonna make him an offer he can't refuse."

Which film is this iconic line from?

A) Goodfellas
B) The Godfather
C) Casino
D) Scarface

Q3. "A census taker once tried to test me. I ate his liver with some fava beans and a nice Chianti."

Who delivers this chilling line?

A) Norman Bates in Psycho
B) Hannibal Lecter in The Silence of the Lambs
C) Patrick Bateman in American Psycho
D) Anton Chigurh in No Country for Old Men

Q4. "I'm going to take my talents to South Beach."

Which athlete made this controversial announcement?

A) Dwyane Wade
B) Chris Bosh
C) LeBron James
D) Shaquille O'Neal

Q5. True or False

"I'm not a crook" was uttered by Ronald Reagan during the Iran-Contra scandal.

Q6. True or False

"The lady's not for turning" was uttered by Margaret Thatcher during a speech defending her economic policies.

Q7. "Mr. Gorbachev, tear down this wall!"

In what context was this famous line delivered?

A) Film
B) Speech
C) Novel
D) TV Show

Q8. Who Am I?

I told graduates to "Stay hungry, stay foolish." I believed "innovation distinguishes between a leader and a follower." I wore the same outfit daily. I said "design is not just what it looks like, design is how it works." I revolutionized phones, computers, and music. I dropped out of college. My garage became legendary. Who am I?

Q9. Unscramble the Slogan and Name the Company

1. "Worth You're Because It"
2. "Machine Driving Ultimate The"
3. "It Do Just"
4. "Mouth Your In Melts Hand Your Not In"
5. "News Print Fit The All To That's"

Q10. Match the Quote to the Film

Match each quote (1-6) with its film (A-F):

Quotes:

1. "Gentlemen, you can't fight in here. This is the war room."
2. "Say hello to my little friend!"
3. "Nobody puts Baby in a corner."
4. "I am serious... and don't call me Shirley."
5. "I love the smell of napalm in the morning."
6. "My name is Inigo Montoya. You killed my father. Prepare to die."

Films:

A) Scarface
B) Airplane!
C) Dirty Dancing
D) Dr. Strangelove or: How I Learned to Stop Worrying and Love the Bomb
E) The Princess Bride
F) Apocalypse Now

Did You Know? The Day the Music Died

On February 3, 1959, at 1:05 AM, a small Beechcraft Bonanza nose-dived into Albert Juhl's frozen cornfield eight miles northwest of Clear Lake, Iowa. The impact killed three of rock and roll's brightest stars instantly. Buddy Holly, still wearing his thick-rimmed glasses, was thrown 40 feet from the wreckage.

Ritchie Valens, just 17 and terrified of flying, had won a coin toss for the seat that killed him. J.P. "The Big Bopper" Richardson, suffering from the flu, had begged Waylon Jennings to swap places so he could stretch out his 6-foot-2 frame instead of cramming into another tour bus seat. The three musicians were traveling between concert dates during what promoters cheerfully called the Winter Dance Party tour, a name that would haunt everyone involved.

What was supposed to be a celebration of music's new energy became its first major tragedy, carved into Iowa farmland by twisted metal and dreams cut short.

The Plane That Changed Everything

For three weeks, the musicians had endured a nightmare tour across the frozen Midwest. Their bus had no heating system, broken windows that let in subzero air, and seats that felt like church pews. Band members were getting frostbite and falling sick from the brutal conditions. Holly, who'd grown up poor in Texas and knew what misery looked like, finally snapped. He chartered a four-seat Beechcraft Bonanza for $36 per person to fly the 365 miles from Clear Lake, Iowa, to their next gig in Moorhead, Minnesota.

The 21-year-old pilot, Roger Peterson, had logged 711 flight hours but wasn't certified for instrument flying. At 12:55 AM, he took off into a blizzard with near-zero visibility, light snow, and 20-mph winds. The temperature was 18 degrees below zero. Four minutes later, the plane was buried nose-first in Albert Juhl's cornfield. In 1959, rock and roll still felt like a teenage rebellion that adults expected would flame out naturally. The crash made brutally clear that the stakes were life and death.

Don McLean's 8½-Minute Memorial

Twelve years later, Don McLean turned that February night into the longest number one hit in Billboard history. "American Pie" wasn't just mourning three dead musicians. It was examining how the optimism of the 1950s had curdled into the chaos of the late 1960s, using the plane crash as the dividing line between innocence and experience.

McLean packed the song with coded references that read like a decade's worth of cultural obituaries. When he sang about "the three men I admire most," listeners heard both the Holy Trinity and the assassinated trinity of John F. Kennedy, Robert Kennedy, and Martin Luther King Jr. The "church bells were all broken" suggested America's lost faith in traditional institutions.

His mention of "Helter Skelter in a summer swelter" directly invoked Charles Manson's twisted interpretation of The Beatles' song, which he used to justify his murderous rampage in 1969. The line about "ten years we've been on our own" marked the exact decade between Holly's death and the song's creation, capturing a generation that felt culturally orphaned. References to marching bands refusing to yield evoked anti-war protests and possibly the Kent State shootings, where National Guard troops fired on student demonstrators. Even his nod to "the book of love" harked back to The Monotones' 1957 hit, representing the innocent doo-wop era that seemed impossibly distant by 1971.

The chorus became a generational anthem, even though most people couldn't decode half the verses. Radio DJs initially refused to play an 8½-minute folk song, but audiences demanded the complete version with all its cryptic storytelling intact.

The Song That Won't Die

McLean called his creation "a morality song" about America losing its way, but for anyone turning 60 in 2025, it was something more personal. You were seven years old when "American Pie" dominated radio in 1972, singing along to words you couldn't possibly understand.

McLean had excavated the cultural wreckage of your earliest years, turning the assassinations, riots, and social upheaval that shaped your childhood into an 8½-minute time capsule. You probably memorized every word while riding in the backseat of your parents' station wagon, long before you understood that "the jester" wasn't actually about medieval entertainment or that February made McLean so sad because it killed his musical heroes, not because of seasonal depression.

The song's reach extends far beyond its original 1971 release. From Tyson Fury's post-fight serenade in a boxing ring to its appearances in Marvel blockbusters, McLean's epic keeps finding new audiences.

A Broadway musical adaptation is in development, because apparently eight and a half minutes of cryptic folk-rock makes perfect theater material. Meanwhile, the Iowa crash site attracts music pilgrims who leave guitar picks and handwritten lyrics in the snow, treating a cornfield like a shrine. At 60, you've lived through enough election cycles and cultural upheavals to suspect that the "simpler times" McLean mourned were probably just as messy as today, only with fewer cameras around to document the chaos.

Round 1 Answers

Time to see if your memory's quotable, or just forgettable.

Q1. Answer: scream, Watson, chocolates, Force, kid

"In space no one can hear you scream" from Alien (1979) became one of cinema's most effective taglines. Space isn't just scary, it's utterly indifferent to your terror. "Elementary, my dear Watson" never appears in Arthur Conan Doyle's original Sherlock Holmes stories. Holmes says "Elementary" separately and calls Watson "my dear Watson," but never in that exact combination. It appeared in early film adaptations and stuck, a Mandela effect before we had a name for it.

"Life is like a box of chocolates" from Forrest Gump (1994). In the original novel, Forrest compares life to cookies, not chocolates. "May the Force be with you" from Star Wars (1977) became the franchise's signature blessing. Many remember Vader saying "Luke, I am your father" but the actual line is "No, I am your father." Our brains fill in context that wasn't there. "Here's looking at you, kid" from Casablanca (1942). Bogart's Rick says this to Bergman's Ilsa, the ultimate bittersweet goodbye.

Q2. Answer: B) The Godfather

Marlon Brando's Don Vito Corleone delivers this in the opening scene. We never actually see him make this "offer," the threat works entirely through implication. The Godfather popularized the idea that the most powerful threats are the ones left unsaid.

Q3. Answer: B) Hannibal Lecter in The Silence of the Lambs

Anthony Hopkins won an Oscar for just 16 minutes of screen time. The "fava beans and Chianti" detail isn't random, it's medically accurate. People on certain psychiatric medications (MAOIs) must avoid those specific foods because they cause dangerous reactions. Lecter's implying he's been off his meds.

Hopkins improvised the famous slurping sound after delivering the line, a creepy flourish that made Jodie Foster's visible discomfort completely genuine. Director Jonathan Demme kept the take because her reaction was so authentic. The actor based Lecter's unsettling voice on a combination of

Truman Capote and Katharine Hepburn, creating that peculiar cultured hiss that made every word feel like a threat wrapped in etiquette.

The role nearly went to Sean Connery, who turned it down calling the script "disgusting." Gene Hackman was also considered but backed out, uncomfortable with the darkness. Hopkins accepted within hours of reading the script. He studied FBI interviews with serial killers and noticed they rarely blinked, so he adopted that predatory stare that made audiences squirm. His preparation paid off: despite appearing in only four scenes totaling 16 minutes across a 118-minute film, he dominated every frame and walked away with the Oscar for Best Actor in 1992.

Q4. Answer: C) LeBron James

LeBron announced "I'm taking my talents to South Beach" on a 2010 televised special called "The Decision," leaving Cleveland for Miami. The phrase became infamous for personalizing a business decision. He returned to Cleveland in 2014 and won them a championship in 2016, somewhat redeeming the departure.

Q5. Answer: FALSE

Richard Nixon said "I'm not a crook" in 1973 during Watergate, not Reagan during Iran-Contra. Nixon was defending himself against accusations he profited from office. He resigned less than a year later. Reagan was never directly implicated in Iran-Contra to the point of making such a defensive statement.

Q6. Answer: TRUE

Thatcher said this at the 1980 Conservative Party Conference, pushing back against critics who wanted her to reverse course on strict economic policies during a recession. "Turn" was a play on "U-turn" (reversing policy). It became her defining statement of political will.

Q7. Answer: B) Speech

Reagan delivered this at the Brandenburg Gate in West Berlin on June 12, 1987, challenging Gorbachev to demolish the Berlin Wall. Two years later, the wall fell. While it's debated how much Reagan's words directly influenced this, the speech became symbolic of the Cold War's end.

Q8. Answer: Steve Jobs

Jobs delivered "Stay hungry, stay foolish" at Stanford's 2005 commencement, quoting the final message from the Whole Earth Catalog. The garage he started Apple in with Wozniak is now a historical site. His daily black turtleneck was inspired by Sony employees' uniforms.

Q9. Answer: "Because You're Worth It" → L'Oréal, "The Ultimate Driving Machine" → BMW, "Just Do It" → Nike, "Melts In Your Mouth Not In Your Hand" → M&M's, "All The News That's Fit To Print" → The New York Times

L'Oréal launched their slogan in 1971, empowering for its time. BMW's has been used since 1973, emphasizing performance. Nike created "Just Do It" in 1988, inspired by death row inmate Gary Gilmore's last words "Let's do it." M&M's introduced theirs in 1954, highlighting the candy shell. The New York Times adopted their motto in 1897, a jab at sensationalist papers.

Q10. Answer: D, A, C, B, F, E

Dr. Strangelove's "you can't fight in here, this is the War Room" captures the absurdity of worrying about etiquette during nuclear war. Scarface's "say hello to my little friend" is Tony Montana's last stand with his M16. Dirty Dancing's "nobody puts Baby in a corner" is Patrick Swayze defending Baby's independence. Airplane!'s "don't call me Shirley" is Leslie Nielsen's deadpan comedy gold. Apocalypse Now's "I love the smell of napalm in the morning" shows Lt. Col. Kilgore finding beauty in chaos. The Princess Bride's "hello, my name is Inigo Montoya" is patient revenge years in the making.

The best quotes are little time machines. Hear "say hello to my little friend" and you're instantly transported back to the first time you saw Scarface, or that friend who wouldn't stop quoting it for months. The ones we remember aren't trying too hard.

They're either weirdly specific (fava beans and Chianti), perfectly timed (don't call me Shirley), or sound exactly like something that person would say. We quote them because they give us shorthand for expressing something, whether it's confidence, humor, or nostalgia for a film we love.

Round 2 – Bands on the run

Paul McCartney once sang about "Band on the Run", but this round is less about dodging prison guards in Lagos and more about chasing down riffs, names, and legacies. Tune your brain like a guitar string and let's see if it stays in key.

Q1. Match the First Names with the Bands

Match each group of first names (A-G) with the correct band (1-7):

A) Paul, John, George, Ringo
B) Ozzy, Tony, Geezer, Bill
C) Mick, Keith, Charlie, Ronnie
D) Freddie, Brian, Roger, John
E) Agnetha, Björn, Benny, Anni-Frid
F) Don, Glenn, Joe, Timothy
G) Stevie, Lindsey, Christine, Mick, John

Bands:

1. Fleetwood Mac
2. The Beatles
3. ABBA
4. The Rolling Stones
5. The Eagles

6. Black Sabbath
7. Queen

Q2. The Dark Side Sync

Pink Floyd's The Dark Side of the Moon spent over 14 years on the Billboard charts, becoming a permanent resident of record collections. Which quirky phenomenon is it most famously (and very unofficially) synced with, especially whispered about by stoners and hippies?

A) Charlie Chaplin's Modern Times
B) Disney's Fantasia
C) The Wizard of Oz
D) The Apollo 11 moon landing footage

Q3. Match the Albums with the Bands

Match each album (A-F) with the correct band (1-6):

A) Nevermind
B) Automatic for the People
C) (What's the Story) Morning Glory?
D) Dookie
E) No Need to Argue
F) The Bends

Bands:

1. R.E.M.
2. Radiohead
3. Oasis
4. Nirvana
5. The Cranberries
6. Green Day

Q4. Iggy Pop's Band

Iggy Pop was the vocalist for which punk rock band?

A) The Clash
B) Sex Pistols

C) Ramones
D) The Stooges

Q5. Rolling Stones Longevity

The Rolling Stones have been performing together for over 60 years. Which original member died in 2021, ending the longest-running lineup in rock history?

A) Brian Jones
B) Charlie Watts
C) Bill Wyman
D) Ian Stewart

Q6. Birthplace of Grunge

Grunge music exploded in the late 1980s and early 1990s, with bands like Nirvana, Pearl Jam, and Soundgarden leading the charge. Which U.S. city is most famously known as the birthplace of grunge?

A) Los Angeles
B) Seattle
C) Chicago
D) Portland

Q7. True or False

The band name KISS is an acronym for Knights in Satan's Service.

Q8. Glastonbury Pyramid Stage Headliners

These bands have all headlined the Pyramid Stage at Glastonbury Festival multiple times. Match each band (1-7) with their headline years (A-G):

Bands:

1. Van Morrison
2. Coldplay
3. The Cure
4. Elvis Costello
5. Arctic Monkeys
6. Muse

7.   Radiohead

Headline years:

A) 2007, 2013, 2023
B) 1986, 1990, 1995, 2019
C) 2002, 2005, 2011, 2016, 2024
D) 1984, 1987, 1989, 1994, 2005, 2013
E) 1982, 1987, 1989, 1992, 1993, 1994, 1997, 2005
F) 2004, 2010, 2016
G) 1997, 2003, 2017

Q9. Who Am I? (Riddle)

Two men at the helm, with jazz-rock blends,
Donald and Walter, lifelong friends.
Reelin' in the Years and Rikki Don't Lose That Number,
Songs to make brainy fans think, not slumber.
Named for a novel's outrageous toy,
They crafted slick albums with wit and joy.
So tell me, dear reader, name the band.

Q10. The 1975

The band "The 1975" took their name from:

A) The year the lead singer was born
B) A date scribbled on the back of a book of poetry
C) The year punk rock started
D) A bus route number in Manchester

Round 2 Answers

Time to face the music. Count your hits, admit your misses, and see if you rocked or flopped.

Q1. Match the First Names with the Bands

A-2 (The Beatles: Paul McCartney, John Lennon, George Harrison, Ringo Starr)
B-6 (Black Sabbath: Ozzy Osbourne, Tony Iommi, Geezer Butler, Bill Ward)
C-4 (The Rolling Stones: Mick Jagger, Keith Richards, Charlie Watts, Ronnie Wood)
D-7 (Queen: Freddie Mercury, Brian May, Roger Taylor, John Deacon)
E-3 (ABBA: Agnetha Fältskog, Björn Ulvaeus, Benny Andersson, Anni-Frid Lyngstad)
F-5 (The Eagles: Don Henley, Glenn Frey, Joe Walsh, Timothy B. Schmit)
G-1 (Fleetwood Mac: Stevie Nicks, Lindsey Buckingham, Christine McVie, Mick Fleetwood, John McVie)

Q2. Answer: C) The Wizard of Oz

The "Dark Side of the Rainbow" is the fan theory that Pink Floyd's album syncs perfectly with the 1939 film when you start the music at the third MGM lion roar. Supposed coincidences include the song "Brain Damage" playing during the Scarecrow's appearance and "The Great Gig in the Sky" matching Dorothy's tornado scene. Pink Floyd has denied any intentional connection, but that hasn't stopped generations of stoned college students from trying it.

Given Pink Floyd's psychedelic reputation and the fact that people have been dropping acid to their music since the '60s, this theory was inevitable. Whether it actually syncs or you just *think* it does probably depends on what you took before pressing play.

Q3. Match the Albums with the Bands

A-4 (Nevermind by Nirvana)
B-1 (Automatic for the People by R.E.M.)
C-3 ((What's the Story) Morning Glory? by Oasis)
D-6 (Dookie by Green Day)
E-5 (No Need to Argue by The Cranberries)
F-2 (The Bends by Radiohead)

These albums defined the 1990s alternative rock scene. Nevermind brought grunge to the mainstream in 1991. Automatic for the People showed R.E.M. at their most vulnerable. Morning Glory made Oasis global superstars in the Britpop wars. Dookie brought punk back to pop radio. No Need to Argue featured "Zombie," written by Dolores O'Riordan about the 1993 Warrington bombings where two children were killed by the IRA, one of the decade's most powerful protest songs against violence in Northern Ireland. The Bends set up Radiohead's later experimental era.

The Warrington bombing killed Tim Parry (12) and Johnathan Ball (3) when IRA members detonated bombs in trash bins. O'Riordan was so disturbed by children dying in sectarian violence that she wrote "Zombie" as an anti-violence anthem, criticizing how the conflict perpetuated cycles of hatred across generations with the line "it's the same old theme since 1916.

Q4. Answer: D) The Stooges

Iggy Pop fronted The Stooges (originally just "The Stooges," later "Iggy and the Stooges") from 1967. They're considered one of the founding bands of punk rock, even though they predated the movement by several years. Iggy's wild stage performances, including self-harm and crowd-diving, influenced every punk frontman who came after. The Stooges weren't commercially successful at first but became massively influential.

Q5. Answer: B) Charlie Watts

Charlie Watts died August 24, 2021, at 80 years old, ending the Rolling Stones' longest-running lineup. He'd been the band's drummer since 1963, 58 years straight. Watts was the quiet, elegant one who wore suits while Mick and Keith descended into rock star chaos. He famously punched Jagger in 1984 after Mick drunkenly called him "my drummer" at 5am. Watts replied "you're my fucking singer" and decked him.

Brian Jones died in 1969, drowning in his swimming pool. Bill Wyman quit in 1993 after 31 years. Ian Stewart was kicked out of the official lineup in 1963 for not looking rock and roll enough but stayed as their road manager and pianist until his death in 1985. The Stones replaced Watts with Steve Jordan and keep touring, because apparently billionaires never retire.

Q6. Answer: B) Seattle

Seattle is the undisputed birthplace of grunge. The scene grew out of the city's underground music community in the mid-1980s, with bands like Nirvana, Pearl Jam, Soundgarden, and Alice in Chains all emerging from the Pacific Northwest. Sub Pop Records, based in Seattle, helped launch many of these bands. The rainy, gray weather supposedly contributed to the music's darker, heavier sound.

Q7. Answer: FALSE

This is one of rock's most persistent myths, but it's completely false. KISS has repeatedly stated the name doesn't stand for anything, it's just a word that looked good and sounded powerful. Gene Simmons and Paul Stanley chose it because it was simple and memorable.

The "Knights in Satan's Service" backronym was created by religious groups in the 1980s during the Satanic Panic. This was a moral panic where parents and religious organizations became convinced that heavy metal, Dungeons & Dragons, and even Saturday morning cartoons were secretly indoctrinating kids into devil worship. KISS, with their makeup and fire-breathing stage shows, became an easy target. The rumor spread so widely that the band had to repeatedly deny it, but conspiracy theories don't need facts to survive.

Q8. Answer: 1-E, 2-C, 3-B, 4-D, 5-A, 6-F, 7-G

Van Morrison: 1982, 1987, 1989, 1992, 1993, 1994, 1997, 2005 (8 times)
Coldplay: 2002, 2005, 2011, 2016, 2024 (5 times)
The Cure: 1986, 1990, 1995, 2019 (4 times)
Elvis Costello: 1984, 1987, 1989, 1994, 2005, 2013 (6 times)
Arctic Monkeys: 2007, 2013, 2023 (3 times)
Muse: 2004, 2010, 2016 (3 times)
Radiohead: 1997, 2003, 2017 (3 times)

Glastonbury is basically the UK's Coachella, except muddier, older, and with way more hippies. It's been running since 1970 on a farm in Somerset, England. Van Morrison holds the record with eight Pyramid Stage headlines spanning 23 years, which is wild considering most bands are lucky to headline once. Coldplay's five slots make them the modern era champions. Elvis Costello's six appearances included some that weren't full headline performances, but he's still festival royalty. The spacing of the years shows how Glastonbury works, bands don't headline back-to-back, they earn their way back over time.

Q9. Answer: Steely Dan

Donald Fagen and Walter Becker formed Steely Dan in 1971. The band name comes from a steam-powered dildo in William S. Burroughs' novel Naked Lunch. Known for perfectionism in the studio, they used session musicians extensively and crafted some of the most musically complex rock albums of the '70s.

Their songs have been used in everything from The Sopranos to The Royal Tenenbaums to Superbad to One Battle After Another. Steely Dan tracks usually show up in movies and TV shows to signal a smooth, sophisticated vibe with a slight edge of cynicism or nostalgia. Whether it's a crime drama, coming-of-age film, or dark comedy, their jazz-influenced sound fits perfectly when you need that "cool but complicated" atmosphere.

Q10. Answer: B) A date scribbled on the back of a book of poetry

Lead singer Matt Healy found a beat poetry book with "1 June, The 1975" scribbled on the back. He thought it sounded cool and evocative without meaning anything specific. The band has said they like that the name doesn't box them into a particular era or genre. It's deliberately vague but still feels like it means something personal.

Round 3 – Reasoning Rumble

Here comes the round where logic tangles itself into knots tighter than your headphones in a pocket. Ducks stand in lines, liars cancel each other out, and Russian roulette gets mathy.

Q1. Duck Dilemma

There are two ducks in front of a duck, two ducks behind a duck, and a duck in the middle. How many ducks are there in total?

Q2. The Fork in the Road

You're at a fork in the road. One direction leads to the City of Lies (where everyone always lies) and the other to the City of Truth (where everyone always tells the truth). There's a person at the fork who lives in one of the cities, but you don't know which one. What single question could you ask them to find out which road leads to the City of Truth?

Q3. The Farmer's Crossing

A farmer wants to cross a river with a wolf, a goat, and a cabbage. His boat can only fit himself plus one other thing at a time. Here's the problem:

- If the wolf and goat are alone together, the wolf eats the goat
- If the goat and cabbage are alone together, the goat eats the cabbage

How can the farmer get everything across the river safely?

Q4. Mystery Number

Find the number based on these clues:

- The number is even
- The number is greater than 10 but less than 20
- The number is not divisible by 4
- The number's digits add up to 5

What's the number?

Q5. Liar, Liar

Three people make the following statements:

- A says: "B is a liar"
- B says: "C is a liar"
- C says: "B is a liar"

Who is telling the truth?

Q6. Drink Detective

Three friends (Anna, Ben, and Carla) each ordered a different drink: tea, coffee, or juice.

- Anna did not order tea
- Ben hates juice

Who had which drink?

Q7. Russian Roulette - Round One

A bad guy is playing Russian roulette with a six-shooter revolver. He puts in one bullet, spins the chambers, and fires at you, but no bullet comes out. He gives you the choice: should he spin the chambers again before firing a second time, or just pull the trigger?

What should you choose?

Q8. Russian Roulette - Round Two

Same situation as Q7, but this time two bullets are loaded in consecutive chambers. After the first shot (which was empty), should you tell him to spin the chambers again or not?

Q9. Tennis Bet

Susan and Lisa decided to play tennis against each other. They bet $1 on each game they played. Susan won three games and Lisa won $5 overall. How many games did they play in total?

Q10. The Letter Mystery

A teacher writes six words on a board: "cat dog has max dim tag"

She gives three students (Albert, Bernard, and Cheryl) each a piece of paper with one letter from one of the words.

She asks Albert, "Do you know the word?" He immediately says yes.

She asks Bernard, "Do you know the word?" He thinks for a moment, then says yes.

She asks Cheryl the same question. She thinks, then says yes.

What is the word?

Did You Know? The Walkman Revolution

A child tears away the sleek packaging to reveal Sony's TPS-L2, smaller than a hardcover book and weighing just over a pound. The device itself was deceptively simple, a silver and blue rectangle with chunky mechanical buttons labeled PLAY, STOP, FAST FORWARD, and REWIND. Two mini headphone jacks sat side by side, allowing friends to share the experience, while a single cassette slot waited hungrily for musical fuel. The foam-padded headphones, lightweight and surprisingly comfortable, completed the package with their distinctive orange sponge earpieces that would become the decade's most recognizable fashion accessory.

The magic happened the moment you pressed play. Your favorite album, previously confined to living room speakers or car stereos, suddenly became portable. The music didn't just play; it followed you, creating an invisible cocoon of sound that transformed ordinary spaces into personal concert venues. Walking to school, riding the bus, even doing chores became opportunities for private musical experiences that no adult could control or interrupt.

In July 1979, Sony introduced a gadget that would define a generation and fundamentally alter the relationship between humans and their soundtracks. The Walkman wasn't just a product launch but a cultural earthquake disguised as consumer electronics. For the first time in history, music became truly portable, liberating millions from the tyranny of shared listening experiences and creating the template for our modern age of personal audio bubbles.

The Great Escape

Before the Walkman, music was a communal affair whether you liked it or not. Families gathered around living room stereos like campfires, forced to negotiate musical taste through democratic suffering or parental dictatorship. Car journeys meant enduring whatever the driver chose, and teenagers were hostages to their parents' easy listening preferences. The Walkman changed this power dynamic overnight, giving individuals the ability to curate their own reality with a simple click of a cassette.

The liberation was intoxicating. Suddenly, joggers could pound pavements to "Eye of the Tiger" instead of the sound of their own labored breathing. Students discovered they could make even the most tedious homework bearable with a Bon Jovi soundtrack. Commuters transformed mundane train rides into personal concerts, nodding along to beats only they could hear. The sight of someone wearing those distinctive lightweight foam headphones became the universal symbol of the 1980s: someone who had opted out of the shared world in favor of their own carefully chosen soundtrack.

The Anxiety of Choice

Parents, predictably, worried that their children were "tuning out" reality, a concern that sounds quaint in an era of smartphones and constant connectivity. The fear wasn't entirely unfounded. Sociologist Murray Schafer had been documenting the world's "soundscape" since the 1960s, arguing that industrial noise pollution was drowning out natural acoustic environments and fundamentally changing how humans related to their surroundings. The Walkman, ironically, offered both escape from this cacophony and contribution to it.

What parents didn't realize was that the Walkman represented something more profound than mere teenage rebellion. It was the first hint of our digital future, where every individual could become their own program director, DJ, and audience of one. The device introduced what media theorist Paul Virilio would later call "dromology," the idea that speed and technology compress human experience in ways that fundamentally alter perception. Suddenly, the rhythm of walking could be divorced from the natural cadence of footsteps and synchronized to whatever beat pulsed through those orange foam earpieces.

The technology sparked an entire ecosystem of behaviors that seem obvious now but were revolutionary then. Mixtape culture exploded as people discovered the joy of sequential storytelling through song selection, creating what academics now recognize as early forms of playlist curation and personal narrative construction. The art of the perfectly timed cassette flip became a skill worth mastering, a tactile ritual that connected the physical act of music consumption to its emotional impact. Friends bonded over shared earbuds, creating intimate musical moments that couldn't be replicated by any stereo system, no matter how expensive. These shared listening experiences became a new form of social intimacy, requiring physical proximity while simultaneously creating psychological distance from the surrounding world.

The mixtape tradition established patterns that would resurface decades later in digital form. Today's Spotify playlists serve the same emotional function as those carefully crafted cassettes, complete with the same anxiety over track sequencing and the same hopes that your musical choices might reveal something meaningful about your inner life to others. The algorithm-driven "Discover Weekly" attempts to replicate what friends once did by sharing their favorite discoveries through homemade compilations, though whether artificial intelligence can match the intimacy of someone physically handing you a tape remains debatable.

From Streets to Streams

Sony's 385 million units sold over three decades established the template for every personal audio device that followed, but the Walkman's influence extends far beyond hardware sales figures. The device fundamentally altered how humans navigate public spaces by creating what urban planners now call "selective engagement" with city environments. Commuters could transform subway rides from communal endurance tests into private retreats. Joggers no longer had to synchronize their pace with the natural rhythm of footsteps or street sounds.

The Walkman also created the first widespread experience of "performative consumption," where previously private musical tastes became visible public statements. Your choice of cassette tape, visible through the clear plastic window, broadcast cultural affiliations to strangers. Headphone brands became status symbols. The sight of someone nodding along to an unknown beat turned music from a shared experience into a form of social theater where others could only guess at the performance.

This shift from communal to individual media consumption accelerated with each technological generation, fundamentally altering how families and communities shared cultural experiences. Before the Walkman, listening to music was inherently social. Families gathered around radio programs at specific times, creating shared memories around the same songs, the same DJ commentary, the same commercial jingles. Record players in living rooms meant everyone heard your music choices, for better or worse. Car trips required negotiation over radio stations, creating a small-scale democracy where musical taste had to be defended and compromises reached.

The Walkman shattered this system by making music consumption a private affair. Suddenly, a teenager could listen to punk rock while their parents remained blissfully unaware three feet away. The shared soundtrack of daily life began fragmenting into millions of individual playlists. This personalization felt liberating, but it also marked the beginning of what sociologists call "lifestyle segregation," where people increasingly surrounded themselves only with media that confirmed their existing preferences rather than challenged them.

Each technological generation accelerated this trend. The Discman offered superior sound quality but required anti-skip protection for movement. The iPod's vast storage eliminated the need to choose which albums to carry but introduced the paralysis of infinite choice. Streaming services promised every song ever recorded but delivered algorithmic suggestions that often felt more like digital fortune-telling than personal curation.

If you're celebrating your 60th birthday in 2025, you witnessed this transformation firsthand. You remember when changing the radio station required walking across the room and turning a dial, when music discovery happened through friends' recommendations rather than algorithmic suggestions.

Did gaining complete control over your audio environment make you more or less open to musical experiences that might surprise you? The Walkman promised freedom from other people's musical choices, but perhaps those involuntary encounters with unfamiliar songs were more valuable than we realized at the time.

Round 3 Answers

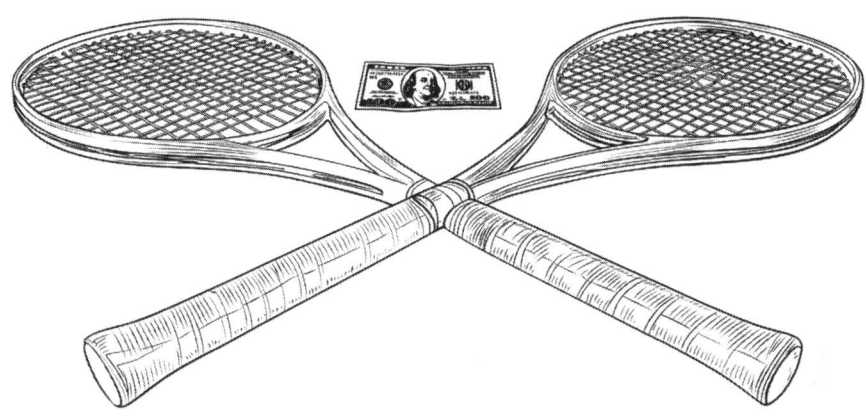

Time to see if you cracked the code like Bletchley Park, or if the Enigma cracked you. Count

Q1. Answer: Three ducks

This is all about perspective. Two ducks are in front of the last duck, the first duck has two ducks behind it, and one duck is in the middle of the other two. They're just standing in a line: Duck 1, Duck 2, Duck 3. Every duck fits the description from a different point of view.

Q2. Answer: "Which direction do you live?"

Both types of people will point to the City of Truth. Someone from the City of Lies will lie about where they live and point to the City of Truth. Someone from the City of Truth will tell the truth and also point to the City of Truth. The question works because it makes the liar's lie cancel itself out.

Q3. Answer: Take the goat first

Step-by-step:

1. Farmer takes goat across (leaves wolf and cabbage, they're safe together)
2. Farmer returns alone
3. Farmer takes wolf across
4. Farmer brings the goat back with him (this is the key move)

31

5. Farmer leaves goat, takes cabbage across
6. Farmer returns alone
7. Farmer takes goat across again

Bringing the goat back on trip 4 is what most people miss. You can bring things back to the starting side.

Q4. Answer: 14

The only number that fits all four clues. It's even, between 10 and 20, not divisible by 4, and 1+4=5. Without that last clue, 18 would also work, but the digits of 18 add up to 9.

Q5. Answer: A and C are telling the truth

If B were honest, then C would be a liar. But C says B is a liar, so if B is honest, C's statement would be a lie, which checks out. But wait: A also says B is a liar. If B is honest, then A is lying too. That means two people are lying and only B is honest? Let's flip it: if B is the liar, then both A and C are telling the truth when they call B out. That works better, two honest people, one liar.

Q6. Answer: Anna = coffee, Ben = tea, Carla = juice

Anna can't have tea, so she's left with coffee or juice. Ben hates juice, so he's stuck with tea or coffee. That means only Carla can have juice without any restrictions. If Carla takes juice, Anna must take coffee (since she can't have tea), leaving Ben with tea. Try it the other way and you get the same result, there's only one combination that works.

Q7. Answer: Yes, make him spin again

Before the first shot, there was a 1 in 6 chance of getting hit. Now that one empty chamber has been used, your odds are 1 in 5 if he doesn't spin, worse odds. If he spins again, you're back to 1 in 6. Always take the better odds.

Q8. Answer: No, don't spin

With two bullets in consecutive chambers, you started with a 2 in 6 chance (or 1 in 3) of getting hit. Since the first shot was empty, that means you're currently in one of four safe positions, and only one of those four is followed by a bullet. That's 1 in 4 odds right now. If you make him spin, you go back to 1 in 3 odds, which is worse. Keep the gun where it is.

Q9. Answer: 11 games

Lisa won $5 overall, but she also lost three games to Susan first. So she was down $3, then had to win those $3 back (3 games), then win another $5 (5 more games). That's 3 losses + 3 wins + 5 wins = 11 games total. The math: Lisa won 8 games ($8) minus Susan's 3 games ($3) = $5 for Lisa.

Q10. Answer: Dog

Albert knows immediately because he has a unique letter (one that only appears once across all six words): c, o, h, s, x, or i. This rules out "tag" right away since both t, a, and g appear multiple times.

Bernard can figure it out from what's left. He knows Albert has a unique letter, so he looks at which words have unique letters. The letters h and s both appear in "has," but all other unique letters are in different words. This eliminates "max" and "dim" for Bernard.

Cheryl can then use the same logic. With "tag," "max," and "dim" ruled out, she's left with "cat," "dog," and "has." Only "dog" has a unique letter that Albert could have gotten right away (the letter "d"). So the word must be "dog."

Logic puzzles work by giving you just enough information that feels like it's not enough, but actually is. Your brain wants more clues when really you just need to think about what each clue eliminates. The best puzzles, like Q10, make you track what other people know, not just what you know.

Round 4 – 80s Movie Magic

The 1980s gave us neon, synths, shoulder pads, and blockbusters that refused to quit. From time-traveling teens to haunted televisions, this round dives into the decade where every film felt like an event, and every soundtrack was waiting to become your mixtape.

Q1. Tagline Time Machine

Match each 1980s movie tagline (A-F) with the film (1-6):

Taglines:

A) "Be afraid. Be very afraid."

B) "He is afraid. He is alone. He is three million light years from home."

C) "They're here"

D) "The first casualty of war is innocence"

E) "Who you gonna call?"

F) "I feel the need... the need for speed"

Films:

1. Ghostbusters (1984)
2. E.T. the Extra-Terrestrial (1982)
3. The Fly (1986)
4. Poltergeist (1982)
5. Platoon (1986)
6. Top Gun (1986)

Q2. Soundtrack Shout-Out

Match each iconic 80s movie song/theme (A-F) with the film (1-6):

Songs/Themes: A) "The Power of Love" by Huey Lewis and the News B) "(I've Had) The Time of My Life" by Bill Medley and Jennifer Warnes C) "Don't You (Forget About Me)" by Simple Minds D) "Footloose" by Kenny

Loggins E) "Eye of the Tiger" by Survivor F) "Take My Breath Away" by Berlin

Films:

1. Top Gun (1986)
2. The Breakfast Club (1985)
3. Dirty Dancing (1987)
4. Back to the Future (1985)
5. Rocky III (1982)
6. Footloose (1984)

Q3. Cast Connection

Match each trio of actors (A-F) with their 1980s film (1-6):

Actor Trios: A) Tom Cruise, Val Kilmer, Anthony Edwards B) Harrison Ford, Sean Young, Rutger Hauer C) Bill Murray, Dan Aykroyd, Harold Ramis D) Matthew Broderick, Alan Ruck, Mia Sara E) Molly Ringwald, Emilio Estevez, Judd Nelson F) Patrick Swayze, Jennifer Grey, Jerry Orbach

Films:

1. Ferris Bueller's Day Off (1986)
2. Ghostbusters (1984)
3. Dirty Dancing (1987)
4. The Breakfast Club (1985)
5. Blade Runner (1982)
6. Top Gun (1986)

Q4. Movie Trivia

In the first Back to the Future film, what year does Marty McFly accidentally travel back to?

A) 1955
B) 1965
C) 1945
D) 1935

Q5. Plot in a Nutshell

Match each quick movie description (A-E) with the film (1-5):

Plots:

A) Teen time travels to 1955, nearly prevents his own birth
B) Five stereotypes spend Saturday detention together, bond over shared angst
C) Slacker fakes sick, steals Ferrari, crashes parade
D) Waxing cars and painting fences is actually karate training
E) Three guys start ghost removal business, fight giant marshmallow man

Films:

1. The Karate Kid (1984)
2. Back to the Future (1985)
3. The Breakfast Club (1985)
4. Ghostbusters (1984)
5. Ferris Bueller's Day Off (1986)

Q6. True or False

In The Terminator, Arnold Schwarzenegger's character says "I'll be back" before smashing through a police station with a car.

Q7. True or False

In Ghostbusters, the team's first paying customer is being haunted by the ghost of her dead husband.

Q8. Director Match

Match each 1980s director (A-F) with their film (1-6):

Directors:

A) John Hughes
B) Robert Zemeckis
C) Steven Spielberg
D) Ridley Scott
E) James Cameron
F) John Carpenter

Films:

1. E.T. the Extra-Terrestrial (1982)
2. The Terminator (1984)
3. Blade Runner (1982)
4. Back to the Future (1985)
5. The Thing (1982)
6. The Breakfast Club (1985)

Q9. Movie Trivia

A manic, improvising comedian plays a military radio DJ who breaks all the rules with his irreverent humor. His signature greeting to listeners became one of the most famous movie catchphrases of the 1980s. What was the catchphrase?

A) "Wake up and smell the napalm!"
B) "Good morning, Vietnam!"
C) "Rise and shine, soldiers!"
D) "This is your wake-up call!"

Q10. Movie Trivia

In Ferris Bueller's Day Off, what type of expensive car do Ferris and Cameron "borrow" from Cameron's father's garage?

A) 1961 Ferrari 250 GT California
B) 1963 Porsche 911
C) 1965 Shelby Cobra
D) 1967 Ford Mustang Fastback

Round 4 Answers

Cue the VHS rewind, let's see if you nailed the 80s or just got stuck tracking lines.

Q1. Answer: A-3, B-2, C-4, D-5, E-1, F-6

"Be afraid. Be very afraid" promoted The Fly's body horror transformation. E.T.'s tagline emphasized the lonely alien's journey home. "They're here" was Poltergeist's simple but creepy announcement. Platoon's tagline reflected Vietnam's impact on young soldiers. Ghostbusters' "Who you gonna call?" became instant pop culture. Top Gun's "need for speed" line became one of the decade's most quoted phrases.

Q2. Answer: A-4, B-3, C-2, D-6, E-5, F-1

"The Power of Love" plays during Back to the Future's skateboard scene. Dirty Dancing's finale wouldn't exist without "(I've Had) The Time of My Life." Simple Minds' track became The Breakfast Club's anthem despite not being written for the film. Kenny Loggins owned 80s soundtracks. "Eye of the Tiger" pumped up Rocky III. Berlin's "Take My Breath Away" soundtracked Top Gun's romance.

Q3. Answer: A-6, B-5, C-2, D-1, E-4, F-3

Top Gun's Maverick, Iceman, and Goose bromance defined the film. Blade Runner's trio carried the neo-noir sci-fi classic. The Ghostbusters core three made comedy and special effects work. Ferris Bueller's trio pulled off the perfect day off. The Breakfast Club ensemble showed Hughes understood teenage angst. Dirty Dancing's three generations created class conflict and romance.

Q4. Answer: A-2, B-3, C-5, D-1, E-4

Back to the Future nearly erased Marty when he cockblocked his own dad. The Breakfast Club's stereotypes learning they're similar became the definitive teen movie. Ferris made hooky look like adventure. Karate Kid's "wax on, wax off" fooled everyone including Daniel-san. Ghostbusters mixed comedy, effects, and Stay Puft Marshmallow Man into box office gold.

Q5. Answer: A-6, B-4, C-1, D-3, E-2, F-5

38

John Hughes owned 80s teen movies. Zemeckis made the DeLorean iconic. Spielberg created cinema's most beloved alien. Ridley Scott's Blade Runner flopped but became a masterpiece. Cameron launched Schwarzenegger's catchphrase career. Carpenter's The Thing remake is now considered better than the original.

Q6. Answer: TRUE

Schwarzenegger delivers the line calmly at the front desk, then returns driving a car through the building. The line became his signature and he's used variations in multiple films. Arnold came up with it himself and writers thought it was too simple, but it became one of cinema's most iconic one-liners.

Q7. Answer: FALSE

Their first customer is a librarian whose library is haunted. No dead husband haunting happens. Slimer becomes one of their most famous catches. The containment unit full of ghosts becomes a plot point when the EPA shuts it down, releasing everything.

Q8. Answer: A) 1955

Marty travels from 1985 to 1955, exactly 30 years back. The year is significant because it's when his parents met at the Enchantment Under the Sea dance. The film uses 1955 to poke fun at 50s culture. Doc Brown needed 1.21 gigawatts to power the flux capacitor.

Q9. Answer: A) 1961 Ferrari 250 GT California

The Ferrari is Cameron's dad's prized possession, making its destruction devastating. Production couldn't afford real Ferraris, so they used replicas. The odometer rolling backward became iconic. Cameron's meltdown over the car crashing through glass is one of the film's most memorable moments.

Q10. Answer: C) Good Morning, Vietnam

Williams improvised most of his radio DJ scenes, with director Barry Levinson letting him riff. The film is based on real DJ Adrian Cronauer's experiences. Williams' manic energy and rapid-fire impressions made the character unforgettable. The movie showed Vietnam from a different perspective, mixing comedy with serious war moments.

Round 5 – Sitcom Central

Sitcoms are comfort food in TV form, equal parts catchphrases, canned laughter, and characters who never seem to learn. Like *Friends*, this round's got plenty of "How you doin'?" energy, except you'll need more answers than Joey ever had.

Q1. Catchphrase Match

Match each catchphrase (A-E) with the sitcom (1-5):

Catchphrases:

A) "That's what she said"

B) "How you doin'?"

C) "Did I do that?"

D) "Yada yada yada"

E) "Bazinga!"

Sitcoms:

1. Friends
2. Seinfeld

3. The Office (US)
4. Family Matters
5. The Big Bang Theory

Q2. Where Are We?

A neighborhood bar in Boston where everybody knows your name. The bartender is a recovering alcoholic and former baseball player. A know-it-all postman and a psychiatrist are regulars. What sitcom is set here?

Q3. Theme Song Scramble

TOLD NO YOU ONE
GONNA LIFE BE WAS
WAY THIS
YOU'RE LIKE ALWAYS IT'S
GEAR STUCK SECOND IN

What sitcom?

Q4. Theme Song Clue

The theme song describes a story about how someone's life got "flipped, turned upside down" and they ended up moving in with wealthy relatives in a California neighborhood. What sitcom?

Q5. Where Are We?

A paper company in Slough, England. The boss is delusional about his management skills and thinks he's a philosopher and entertainer. There's an awkward receptionist being pursued by a warehouse worker while engaged to someone else. What sitcom?

Q6. Multiple Choice

In Seinfeld, what is Kramer's first name?

A) It's never revealed
B) Newman
C) Stanley
D) Cosmo

Q7. Catchphrase to Character

"Norm!" is the greeting that everyone shouts when this character enters the bar in Cheers. What is Norm's full name?

A) Norman Clavin
B) Norman Tortelli
C) Norman Peterson
D) Norman Boyd

Q8. Family Tree Trivia

Three very different families connected by remarriage: a blended family with a widowed father and his three sons, a gay couple with an adopted daughter, and a May-December romance with a much younger Colombian wife and her son. What sitcom?

A) Arrested Development
B) Modern Family
C) Schitt's Creek
D) The Fresh Prince of Bel-Air

Q9. Theme Song Clue

The theme song mentions four women being confidantes, describes them as sharing life's troubles, and references one of them being the eldest. What sitcom about four women living in Miami?

Q10. Fawlty Towers

In Fawlty Towers, what is the name of Basil's long-suffering wife?

A) Sybil
B) Polly
C) Margaret
D) Audrey

Did You Know? Don't Mention the War!

Only 12 episodes long, Fawlty Towers managed to achieve what most sitcoms spend decades trying to accomplish. This British masterpiece about a rude, bumbling hotel owner aired in just two short runs (1975 and 1979) and quit while it was ahead, proving that sometimes it's better to leave the party early than overstay your welcome. The first episode broadcast on September 19, 1975, placing us now exactly half a century away from that moment, as distant as Fawlty Towers was from John Logie Baird's first successful television transmission in 1925. Like the Beatles' music, it became part of the dominant cultural language of its era.

John Cleese's Basil Fawlty was the cranky Torquay innkeeper who could transform a simple hotel booking into a diplomatic incident, whether he was goose-stepping in front of German tourists or berating the perpetually confused waiter Manuel with increasingly frantic Spanish. To rewatch the show today is to be reminded how genuinely appalling Basil really is: sneaky, pompous, pedantic, xenophobic, and an insufferable snob. Yet like Larry David in Curb Your Enthusiasm, he usually has just enough of a point to make his outrageous behavior almost defensible. Almost.

The Real Basil Fawlty

The character's genesis sounds almost too perfect to be true. While filming Monty Python's Flying Circus in 1970, the troupe stayed at the Gleneagles Hotel in Torquay, where they encountered owner Donald Sinclair. Sinclair would wait in the lobby to monitor the Pythons' evening returns and even demonstrated proper British knife-and-fork technique to American member Terry Gilliam. His rudeness was so spectacular it bordered on performance art: throwing bus schedules at guests, hiding behind potted plants to eavesdrop, and once hurling a guest's briefcase out a window because he suspected it contained explosives. It was full of clothes.

Most people would have simply left a scathing review and moved on. Cleese recognized comedy gold and turned Sinclair's real-life awfulness into television history, proving that sometimes the best characters aren't invented but discovered. Sinclair later claimed he was proud to have inspired the show, suggesting either remarkable self-awareness or complete obliviousness to how he was being portrayed.

Less Is More, Much More

The show's brevity was its secret weapon. While American sitcoms were grinding out 22-episode seasons year after year, Cleese and co-creator Connie Booth crafted each half-hour like a Swiss watch of cringe comedy. Every pratfall, every misunderstanding, every moment of Basil's mounting hysteria was precisely calibrated for maximum awkwardness. The opening credits alone became a running gag, with the "Fawlty Towers" hotel sign rearranged into different anagrams each episode: "Warty Towels," "Flowery Twats," "Farty Towels." Even the title sequence warned viewers they were entering a world where nothing worked properly.

Each episode delivered moments of pure comedic genius. Basil's concussion-fueled breakdown in front of German tourists, complete with goose-stepping and frantic shouts of "Don't mention the war!", became sitcom legend. When his car broke down while fetching a gourmet meal, viewers watched him emerge with a tree branch to give the vehicle "a damn good thrashing," cursing at it like a disappointed parent. The physical comedy between Basil and the bewildered Manuel reached absurd heights with constant head slaps and Manuel's insistence that his pet rat was actually "a Siberian hamster," leading to chaos when health inspectors came calling.

The Ancestry of Awkwardness

Decades later, Fawlty Towers' DNA runs through every lovably horrible protagonist on television. From Seinfeld's neurotic narcissists to Larry David's social disasters in Curb Your Enthusiasm, the template remains unchanged: flawed characters making terrible decisions in escalating situations. The show proved that audiences would happily watch people behave badly, provided the writing was sharp enough to make the pain feel worthwhile.

The formula seems simple until you try to replicate it. Most sitcoms that attempt the "awful protagonist" approach end up creating characters who are merely annoying rather than entertainingly dreadful. Basil Fawlty worked because beneath his pompous exterior lay genuine vulnerability and occasional flashes of self-awareness. He wasn't just rude; he was desperately trying to maintain dignity in an undignified world, which made his failures both painful and sympathetic. Whether he was frantically searching for Waldorf salad ingredients while maintaining a professional facade or berating Manuel in increasingly frantic Spanish, Basil's desperation felt authentically human despite its comic excess.

Round 5 Answers

Cue the laugh track, time to see if your answers were comic gold or a canceled pilot.

Q1. Answer: A-3, B-1, C-4, D-2, E-5

Michael Scott's "That's what she said" was improvised by Steve Carell so much that the writers started building it into scripts. Joey's "How you doin'?" became such a trademark that Matt LeBlanc couldn't escape it for years after Friends ended. Steve Urkel wasn't even supposed to be a main character on Family Matters, just a one-time guest, but "Did I do that?" made him so popular they rebuilt the entire show around him. Seinfeld's "yada yada yada" was actually Julia Louis-Dreyfus's idea to skip boring exposition. Sheldon's "Bazinga!" doesn't appear until season 2 of The Big Bang Theory, and Jim Parsons has said he hated saying it by the end.

Q2. Answer: Cheers

The show was nearly canceled after its first season because of terrible ratings. Only 77th out of 100 shows. NBC kept it alive and by season 3 it was a hit. Ted Danson's character Sam was supposed to be a retired football player, but they changed it to baseball because Danson couldn't convincingly throw a football. The bar set was so detailed that cast members would actually drink the beer between takes (it was real). Frasier was only supposed to appear in a few episodes, but Kelsey Grammer's performance was so good he became a main character and eventually got his own spinoff that ran 11 seasons.

Q3. Answer: Friends

Unscrambled: "No one told you life was gonna be this way / It's like you're always stuck in second gear"

The Rembrandts weren't exactly thrilled about becoming "the Friends theme band," but hey, the royalty checks probably softened the blow. The song hit number one and made them rich for life, even if it meant playing it at every single concert forever. Originally just an instrumental track, NBC pushed for lyrics, and it became one of the most recognizable TV themes ever. Not bad for something they initially didn't want to record.

Q4. Answer: The Fresh Prince of Bel-Air

Will Smith was broke and owed the IRS $2.8 million when he got this role. The IRS took 70% of his paycheck for the first three seasons to pay off his tax debt. He actually rapped the entire theme song in one take. If you watch early episodes, you can see him mouthing other actors' lines because he memorized the entire script, not just his own parts.

The Banks' mansion wasn't in Bel-Air at all, it was in Brentwood. Alfonso Ribeiro (Carlton) didn't invent the Carlton Dance, he stole it from Courteney Cox's dancing in a Bruce Springsteen music video and Eddie Murphy's "white guy dance" from his stand-up.

Q5. Answer: The Office (UK)

Ricky Gervais based David Brent on a boss he had at a temp agency who would play guitar at parties and thought everyone loved him. The show only had 14 total episodes but changed comedy forever. BBC almost didn't air the second series because the first one got such low ratings. Stephen Merchant (the co-creator) is 6'7" and appears in several episodes as Oggy, the guy in the warehouse. The Christmas special where Tim and Dawn finally get together made grown adults cry, which nobody expected from a cringe comedy. Martin Freeman (Tim) went straight from this to playing Bilbo in The Hobbit trilogy.

Q6. Answer: D) Cosmo

Kramer's first name wasn't revealed until season 6 because Larry David's real neighbor (who inspired the character) didn't want his name used. Once they settled the rights, boom, Cosmo Kramer. Michael Richards based Kramer's physical comedy on a combination of his own awkwardness and silent film stars. He refused to rehearse the door entrances because he wanted them to feel spontaneous.

Q7. Answer: C) Norman Peterson

George Wendt gained 50 pounds during the show's run because Norm was always drinking beer (real beer for the first few seasons until they switched to near-beer). His wife Vera was mentioned in nearly every episode but never shown on camera, though they did cast her once and shot a scene where you only see her get a pie in the face. The writers gave Norm one-liners whenever he entered the bar, and Wendt would often improvise them. After Cheers ended, Wendt tried to launch a spinoff called "The Tortellis" about Carla's ex-husband's family, but it bombed after 13 episodes.

Q8. Answer: Modern Family

Ty Burrell based Phil Dunphy on optimistic 1980s sitcom dads, especially Alan Thicke in Growing Pains. Sofia Vergara became the highest-paid TV actress by 2012, earning $325,000 per episode.

Q9. Answer: The Golden Girls

Betty White was originally supposed to play Blanche, and Rue McClanahan was supposed to play Rose, but they switched roles at the last minute because the casting director thought it would be more interesting to see them play against type. Estelle Getty (Sophia) was actually younger than Bea Arthur (Dorothy), who played her daughter. The cheesecake scenes weren't scripted at first, the actresses would just eat cheesecake between takes and the writers loved it so much they made it a recurring thing. The lanai set (the wicker furniture area) was so uncomfortable that the actresses complained constantly. NBC executives wanted to cancel it after season one because they thought nobody would watch a show about "old women."

Q10. Answer: A) Sybil

Sybil Fawlty was Basil's domineering wife in *Fawlty Towers*, played by Prunella Scales. The show was inspired by the notoriously rude Donald Sinclair, owner of the Gleneagles Hotel where John Cleese stayed in 1970. Only 12 episodes were made because Cleese refused to compromise quality, and the show later ranked #1 on the BFI's list of Greatest British Television Programmes.

Round 6 – U.S. Power Plays

Think of this as *The West Wing* in quiz form, fast talk, big stakes, and presidents who could fill a whole trivia book on their own.

Q1. Mount Rushmore Math

Four presidents are carved into Mount Rushmore:

- The father of our country who couldn't tell a lie
- The author of the Declaration of Independence who doubled our size
- The Great Emancipator who saved the Union
- The Rough Rider who built the Panama Canal

Add up their president numbers. What's the total?

Q2. Amendment Match

Match each amendment description (A-E) with its number (1-5):

Descriptions:

A) You don't have to let soldiers live in your house during peacetime

B) You can't be tried twice for the same crime

C) Freedom of speech, religion, press, and assembly

D) The right to bear arms

E) No unreasonable searches and seizures

Amendment Numbers:

1. First Amendment
2. Second Amendment
3. Third Amendment
4. Fourth Amendment
5. Fifth Amendment

Q3. Political Portrait

This First Lady launched the "Just Say No" anti-drug campaign in the 1980s as part of the War on Drugs. She was known for her influence over her husband's presidency, consulted astrologers for scheduling decisions, and had a famous feud with her daughter. Who was she?

A) Betty Ford
B) Nancy Reagan
C) Barbara Bush
D) Rosalynn Carter

Q4. President Pop Quiz

This president kept a pet alligator in the White House, won a duel before his presidency (killing his opponent), and survived an assassination attempt when the bullet hit his thick speech manuscript in his coat pocket. Who was he?

A) Andrew Jackson
B) Ulysses S. Grant
C) James K. Polk
D) Zachary Taylor

Q5. Presidential Scandals Fill-in-the-Blank

Fill in the scandal name for each presidential crisis:

A) Nixon authorized a break-in at the Democratic National Committee headquarters at the _____ Hotel, leading to his resignation.

B) Reagan's administration secretly sold arms to Iran and used the profits to fund Contra rebels in Nicaragua, known as the _____ affair.

C) Clinton's affair with a White House intern led to his impeachment for lying under oath. The scandal is known by the intern's last name: the _____ scandal.

D) The _____ Dome scandal under Harding involved bribing government officials for oil drilling rights on federal land.

Q6. Amendment Match

This amendment abolished slavery and involuntary servitude (except as punishment for a crime). What number is it?

A) 13th Amendment
B) 14th Amendment
C) 15th Amendment
D) 16th Amendment

Q7. President Pop Quiz

Match each presidential fact (A-G) with the president (1-7):

Facts:

A) Got stuck in White House plumbing, needed custom furniture made
B) A bullet lodged in his chest didn't stop him from finishing his speech
C) Dueled a man to death, kept exotic pets in the executive mansion
D) Screen star turned politician, cracked jokes while bleeding from gunshot
E) Youngest recipient of a major peace prize for a president
F) Peanut farmer turned peacemaker, helped broker Middle East peace
G) Played the saxophone on late night TV, faced impeachment over an affair

Presidents:

1. Andrew Jackson
2. Theodore Roosevelt
3. William Howard Taft
4. Jimmy Carter
5. Ronald Reagan
6. Bill Clinton

7. Barack Obama

Q8. President Pop Quiz

This president was a Hollywood actor before politics, survived an assassination attempt just 69 days into his presidency, and ended nearly every speech with "God bless America." His economic policies were nicknamed after him. Who was he?

A) Gerald Ford
B) Richard Nixon
C) Ronald Reagan
D) George H.W. Bush

Q9. Election Year Mashup

The Berlin Wall fell and the Tiananmen Square protests happened in China. What U.S. presidential election year was the following year?

A) 1988
B) 1992
C) 1996
D) 2000

Q10. Amendment Match

Women gained the right to vote. What amendment number?

A) 15th Amendment
B) 18th Amendment
C) 19th Amendment
D) 21st Amendment

Round 6 Answers

Like Nixon's tapes, the truth comes out here. Time to check your score.

Q1. Answer: 46

Washington (1st) + Jefferson (3rd) + Lincoln (16th) + Theodore Roosevelt (26th) = 46

Washington is the cherry tree guy and first president. Jefferson wrote the Declaration of Independence and completed the Louisiana Purchase. Lincoln freed the slaves and kept the country from splitting in two during the Civil War. Teddy Roosevelt was a Rough Rider in the Spanish-American War and pushed for the Panama Canal (and basically stole Panama from Colombia to do it). These four were chosen for Mount Rushmore to represent the nation's birth, growth, preservation, and development. Sculptor Gutzon Borglum picked them, not a committee, which is why no women or minorities made the cut despite their contributions.

Q2. Answer: A-3, B-5, C-1, D-2, E-4

Third Amendment (soldiers in houses) almost never comes up in court cases because, well, we don't quarter soldiers in private homes anymore. It was a direct response to British troops forcing colonists to house them before the Revolution. The Fifth Amendment covers way more than just "pleading the fifth," it also includes due process and the government can't take your property without fair compensation. The Fourth Amendment is why cops need warrants, though there are about a million exceptions that have been carved out over the years.

Q3. Answer: B) Nancy Reagan

Nancy Reagan's "Just Say No" campaign became the face of the 1980s War on Drugs, though critics argued it oversimplified addiction and didn't actually help. She appeared on TV shows like Diff'rent Strokes to promote it. The astrology thing was real, she consulted astrologer Joan Quigley to help schedule Reagan's events after the 1981 assassination attempt, which his staff found ridiculous but couldn't stop. Her relationship with daughter Patti Davis was notoriously rocky, with Patti writing tell-all books about the family dysfunction. Nancy was fiercely protective of Ronald and wielded serious power behind the scenes, getting staff fired if she didn't like them.

Q4. Answer: A) Andrew Jackson

Jackson killed Charles Dickinson in an 1806 duel over a horse racing bet and an insult to his wife. Dickinson shot first, hitting Jackson in the chest (the bullet stayed there for life), but Jackson calmly returned fire and killed him. The assassination attempt happened in 1835 when Richard Lawrence tried to shoot him, but both pistols misfired (Jackson then beat him with his cane). The alligator was a gift from the Marquis de Lafayette and supposedly lived in the East Room. Jackson also holds the record for most duels by a president, estimated between 5 and 100 depending on who you ask.

Q5. Answer: A) Watergate, B) Iran-Contra, C) Lewinsky, D) Teapot

Watergate (1972-1974) started with a break-in at Democratic offices and ended with Nixon resigning—the cover-up was worse than the crime. Deep Throat (FBI's Mark Felt) leaked to Woodward and Bernstein. Iran-Contra (1985-1987) involved selling weapons to Iran and using proceeds to fund Nicaraguan Contras, which Congress had banned. Oliver North took the fall, Reagan claimed ignorance, and most involved got pardoned. The Lewinsky scandal (1998-1999) got Clinton impeached for lying under oath about the affair after his famous "I did not have sexual relations with that woman" denial. He was acquitted by the Senate.

Teapot Dome (1921-1923) was the era's biggest scandal: Interior Secretary Albert Fall accepted bribes to lease federal oil reserves to private companies. Fall became the first Cabinet member imprisoned. Harding died before it fully broke.

Q6. Answer: A) 13th Amendment

Ratified in 1865 after the Civil War, the 13th Amendment officially ended slavery in America. The "except as punishment for crime" loophole is why prison labor is still legal and has been heavily criticized as perpetuating slavery under a different name. Some states still had slavery on their books until shockingly recently (Mississippi didn't officially ratify it until 2013, though it had been federally binding since 1865). The amendment passed the House by just two votes.

Q7. Answer: A-3, B-2, C-1, D-5, E-7, F-4, G-6

Taft got stuck in the White House bathtub and needed six men to pull him out; his replacement tub fit four people. Roosevelt took a bullet to the chest in 1912 but delivered his 90-minute speech anyway—his manuscript and glasses case slowed the bullet. Jackson killed a man in a duel over an insult to his wife and carried that bullet in his chest for life; he fought between 5-100 duels total. Reagan joked "I hope you're all Republicans" to surgeons after being shot 69 days into his presidency.

Obama won the Nobel Peace Prize in 2009 after less than a year in office, making him the youngest sitting president to receive it at 47. Carter brokered the Camp David Accords in 1978 and won his own Nobel in 2002. Clinton played saxophone on Arsenio Hall in 1992 and was later impeached for lying under oath about the Lewinsky affair but acquitted by the Senate.

Q8. Answer: C) Ronald Reagan

Reagan was shot by John Hinckley Jr. on March 30, 1981, just 69 days into his presidency. The bullet missed his heart by an inch. His joke to surgeons ("I hope you're all Republicans") became legendary. When he later saw Hinckley's mugshot, he quipped "That guy missed me." His quick wit and Hollywood charm helped him survive the assassination attempt politically as much as medically.

Q9. Answer: B) 1992

The Berlin Wall fell in November 1989, and the Tiananmen Square massacre happened in June 1989. The following presidential election was 1992 (Bush vs. Clinton). This question tests if you remember that presidential elections happen every four years. 1989 was a pivotal year for global politics, marking the beginning of the end of the Cold War. The fall of the Berlin Wall basically symbolized the collapse of Soviet influence in Eastern Europe, while Tiananmen Square showed China's government wasn't about to allow similar democratic movements.

Q10. Answer: C) 19th Amendment

Ratified in 1920 after decades of suffragist activism, protests, hunger strikes, and arrests. Women like Susan B. Anthony, Elizabeth Cady Stanton, and Alice Paul spent their lives fighting for this. Some women could vote in certain states before 1920 (Wyoming gave women the vote in 1869), but the 19th Amendment made it nationwide. It still didn't guarantee voting rights for all women, Black women in the South faced massive barriers until the Voting Rights Act of 1965. The fight took 72 years from the first women's rights convention in 1848 to ratification.

Round 7 – 90s Big Screen Buzz

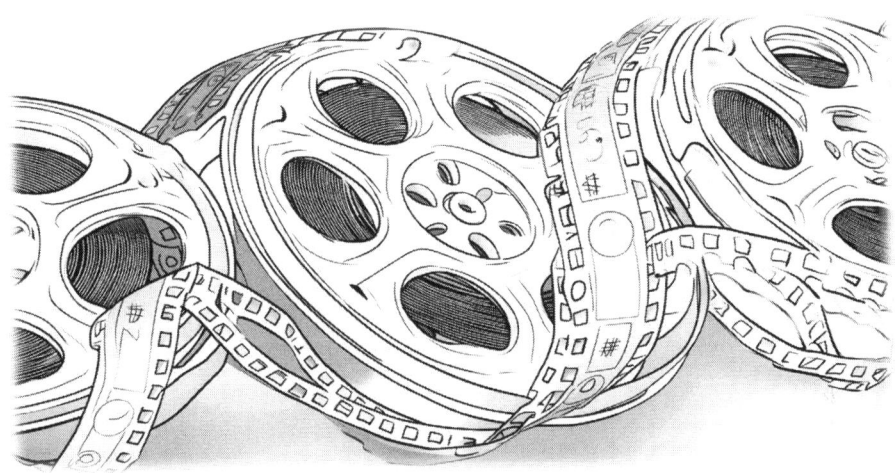

The 90s gave us bullet-time, dinosaurs that actually looked real, and more quotable lines than Blockbuster had late fees. This round is a popcorn bucket full of cinematic chaos, just don't spill it like Newman in *Jurassic Park*.

Q1. Quote This Flick

Match each 90s movie quote (A-E) with the film (1-5):

Quotes:

A) "You can't handle the truth!"

 B) "Life is like a box of chocolates"

C) "I see dead people"

D) "Show me the money!"

E) "I'm not even supposed to be here today!"

Films:

1. Jerry Maguire (1996)
2. The Sixth Sense (1999)
3. A Few Good Men (1992)

4. Forrest Gump (1994)
5. Clerks (1994)

Q2. Profanity Record

Which 1990s crime film contains 269 instances of the word "fuck," placing it among movies with the highest frequency of profanity?

A) Casino
B) Goodfellas
C) Reservoir Dogs
D) The Usual Suspects

Q3. Match the Character to Profession

Match each character (A-E) with their profession (1-5):

Characters:

A) Patrick Bateman
B) Clarice Starling
C) Jules Winnfield
D) Woody
E) Neo

Professions:

1. Computer programmer who discovers he's living in a simulation
2. Cowboy toy who's jealous of a new space ranger
3. FBI trainee hunting a serial killer
4. Investment banker with a violent secret life
5. Hitman who quotes scripture before killing people

Q4. Director Match

Match each 90s director (A-F) with their film (1-6):

Directors:

A) Quentin Tarantino
B) James Cameron
C) M. Night Shyamalan

D) Steven Spielberg
E) The Wachowskis
F) David Fincher

Films:

1. The Matrix (1999)
2. Schindler's List (1993)
3. Titanic (1997)
4. Pulp Fiction (1994)
5. Fight Club (1999)
6. The Sixth Sense (1999)

Q5. Soundtrack Spin

Which 90s movie soundtrack is the best-selling soundtrack of all time?

A) The Bodyguard
B) Forrest Gump
C) Titanic
D) The Lion King

Q6. Who Played Who?

Match each actor/role pairing (A-E) with the film (1-5):

Actor/Role:

A) Tom Hanks as a slow-witted man who witnesses major historical events

B) Brad Pitt as an insomniac's anarchist alter ego

C) Jim Carrey as a man whose entire life is a TV show

D) Robin Williams as a therapist helping a troubled genius

E) Samuel L. Jackson as a philosophical hitman

Films:

1. Good Will Hunting (1997)
2. Fight Club (1999)

3. Pulp Fiction (1994)
4. The Truman Show (1998)
5. Forrest Gump (1994)

Q7. Animated Voice Match

Match each voice actor (A-E) with the 90s animated character they voiced (1-5):

Voice Actors:

A) Val Kilmer
B) Robin Williams
C) Tom Hanks
D) Eddie Murphy
E) James Earl Jones

Characters:

1. Genie in Aladdin
2. Woody in Toy Story
3. Mufasa in The Lion King
4. Moses in The Prince of Egypt
5. Donkey in Shrek

Q8. Quote This Flick

"As far back as I can remember, I always wanted to be a gangster." Which actor narrates this opening line?

A) Ray Liotta in Goodfellas
B) Robert De Niro in Casino
C) Al Pacino in Donnie Brasco
D) Joe Pesci in Goodfellas

Q9. Soundtrack Match

Match each iconic 90s movie song (A-E) with the film (1-5):

Songs:

A) "Where Is My Mind?" by Pixies

B) "You've Got a Friend in Me" by Randy Newman

C) "My Heart Will Go On" by Celine Dion

D) "Iris" by Goo Goo Dolls

E) "Kiss from a Rose" by Seal

Films:

1. Batman Forever (1995)
2. Toy Story (1995)
3. City of Angels (1998)
4. Fight Club (1999)
5. Titanic (1997)

Q10. Who Am I?

I ran across America despite having leg braces as a child. I met three presidents, survived Vietnam, became a ping-pong champion, and inspired a famous running shoe company. My best friend was named after a shrimp boat. My mama always said life was unpredictable, like a certain box of sweets. Who am I?

Did You Know? The Perfect Teenage Fantasy

"Life moves pretty fast. If you don't stop and look around once in a while, you could miss it."

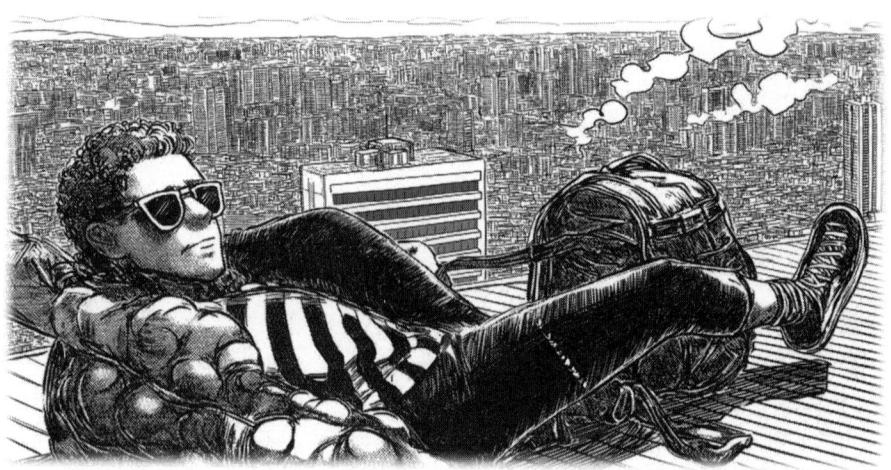

In 1986, Matthew Broderick stepped into the role that would define teenage wish fulfillment for generations. Ferris Bueller wasn't your typical high school rebel. He didn't smoke behind the gym, get into fights, or terrorize freshmen. Instead, he possessed something far more subversive: the ability to make rule-breaking look effortless, charming, and consequence-free. Director John Hughes, fresh off successes with Sixteen Candles and The Breakfast Club, had created the perfect teenage fantasy character, someone who could skip school, commandeer expensive cars, and crash parades without anyone staying mad at him for long. While Hughes's previous films explored teenage angst and social hierarchies, Ferris Bueller represented something entirely different: a teenager who had somehow figured out how to beat the system without becoming bitter about it.

Existential Teenager

Ferris Bueller was considered "deep" because the film uses his character to explore existentialist themes of individuality and freedom against societal norms, and the idea of seizing the moment before life passes by. His revolt against expectations wasn't driven by anger or rebellion for its own sake, but by a philosophical commitment to authentic living. While his classmates dutifully attended economics lectures, Ferris questioned why anyone should spend beautiful spring days trapped indoors when the world offered so much to experience.

This existential approach made him dangerous in a completely different way than traditional teenage rebels. He couldn't be dismissed as a troubled kid acting out because his logic was sound and his methods were surprisingly thoughtful. His famous improvised line about life moving fast wasn't just a throwaway quip but a genuine philosophical statement about the human condition. John Hughes reportedly added this line at the last minute, recognizing it captured the film's core message about embracing fleeting moments rather than postponing happiness.

The Cameron Factor

The film's true depth comes from the transformative effect Ferris has on his anxious friend Cameron, who finds courage and asserts himself against his domineering father, making Cameron the actual hero of the story. Cameron begins the film as a neurotic, hypochondriacal teenager paralyzed by fear of his father's disapproval. Through Ferris's influence, he gradually learns to take risks, express his feelings, and ultimately confront the source of his anxiety in a climactic scene involving his father's prized Ferrari.

Cameron's character arc provides the emotional weight that prevents the film from being merely a lighthearted romp. His struggle with parental expectations and his journey toward self-assertion resonated with audiences who recognized their own fears about disappointing authority figures. The destruction of the Ferrari becomes a symbolic act of liberation, with Cameron finally choosing his own wellbeing over his father's material obsessions.

The Soundtrack of Rebellion

The film's most iconic moment captures everything about Ferris's character in a single scene. During the Von Steuben Day Parade in Chicago, he commandeers a float and lip-syncs to The Beatles' "Twist and Shout," transforming what should have been a modest German-American cultural celebration into a city-wide party. The choice of song was brilliant: a Beatles cover of an Isley Brothers track that had already proven its ability to get crowds moving. Watching Ferris perform, you can see how his infectious joy spreads through the crowd like a virus, turning skeptical bystanders into enthusiastic participants.

This scene works because it taps into something universally appealing about spontaneous public performance. Most people have fantasized about commanding attention in a positive way, about being the person who can turn a mundane moment into something memorable. The parade sequence fulfills that fantasy while showing Ferris's core philosophy in action: why settle for being a passive observer when you could be the main event?

The film's soundtrack extended beyond this centerpiece moment to create a sonic landscape that defined 1980s cool. Yello's "Oh Yeah," with its distinctive synthesized vocals and minimalist electronic beat, became synonymous with luxury and sophistication after appearing during scenes featuring Cameron's father's Ferrari. The song's hypnotic quality matched the car's sleek aesthetics perfectly, creating a sensory connection between sound and status that resonated throughout the decade.

Hughes made Chicago itself a character in the film, using specific locations like Wrigley Field and the Art Institute that locals recognized, and tourists envied. The choice to set the film during a perfect spring day was crucial, anyone who has endured a Midwest winter understands the religious significance of the first beautiful day of spring. The film captures that specific feeling of emerging from months of cold into sunshine and possibility, when skipping school feels like a natural response to meteorological good fortune rather than rebellion.

The Hughes Universe

Hughes populated Ferris Bueller's world with the same attention to teenage social dynamics that marked his other films, but with a crucial difference. While The Breakfast Club examined the painful reality of high school hierarchies and Sixteen Candles explored the awkwardness of adolescent romance, Ferris Bueller presented a fantasy where those systems could be transcended through sheer force of personality. It was Hughes's first teenager who seemed to have read the manual on how high school was supposed to work and decided to ignore it completely.

Jennifer Grey's performance as Ferris's resentful sister Jeannie provided a counterpoint to his effortless success, representing every teenager who couldn't understand why some people seemed to glide through life while others struggled. Her character served as the film's reality check, voicing the frustration that audiences might feel watching someone so seemingly perfect. The dynamic between them reflected real sibling relationships where one child appears to receive all the luck and charisma while the other watches from the sidelines, muttering about cosmic unfairness.

The film's authority figures, particularly Principal Rooney, followed Hughes's established pattern of adults who were either oblivious, incompetent, or actively antagonistic toward teenagers. Rooney's single-minded pursuit of Ferris borders on the obsessive, suggesting that perhaps the real truant from adult responsibilities was the grown man spending an entire day trying to catch one teenager. Unlike Hughes's other films where these adults often had legitimate points about teenage behavior, Ferris Bueller portrayed authority as something to be outwitted rather than confronted or understood. This represented a shift in Hughes's perspective, moving from complex examinations of adult-teenager relationships toward pure teenage wish fulfillment, where adults existed primarily as obstacles to be cleverly circumvented rather than humans with their own valid concerns.

The Timeless Appeal

The film's cultural impact inspired real-world elaborate senior skip days and increased Chicago tourism to its locations. Matthew Broderick's performance launched him to stardom, though he later admitted Ferris's effortless confidence was opposite his naturally anxious personality. The film influenced subsequent teen comedies through direct-to-camera addresses (She's All That, Easy A) and the Spider-Man films borrowed heavily from the Ferris template. Ferris endures because he solved problems that have only worsened—he showed how to be confident without cruelty, popular without shallowness, and rebellious without destruction. In a social media age where every mistake gets documented, his ability to remain genuinely likeable while taking risks feels like a superpower.

Still Taking Days Off

Ferris represents a vanishing breed: the teenager who can improvise adventure from an ordinary day, a freedom largely disappeared in an era of helicopter parenting. He showed how to be confident without cruelty, popular without shallowness, and rebellious without destruction. In a social media age where every mistake gets documented, his ability to remain likeable while taking risks feels like a superpower.

Round 7 Answers

Like Tyler Durden's rules, your score can't stay secret. Time to see if you played this round or just imagined it.

Q1. Answer: A-3, B-4, C-2, D-1, E-5

Jack Nicholson's "You can't handle the truth!" was reportedly inspired by a real-life incident where an audience member heckled him during a play, prompting an equally explosive, off-script retort. Tom Hanks made Forrest's chocolate wisdom instantly quotable. Haley Joel Osment's whispered "I see dead people" became the twist everyone knew before seeing the film. Cuba Gooding Jr. screaming at Tom Cruise defined Jerry Maguire's desperation. Dante's complaint in Clerks became the rallying cry for every retail worker stuck on their day off.

Q2. Answer: C) Reservoir Dogs

Tarantino's budget was so small he couldn't afford enough fake blood. When Mr. Orange (Tim Roth) is shot and bleeding profusely on the floor, the crew used maple syrup mixed with food coloring for some of the blood effects. The entire film takes place mostly in one warehouse with guys in suits arguing and bleeding. It launched Tarantino's career and proved sharp dialogue plus extreme violence could work on a tiny budget. Casino and Goodfellas came close with their own impressive profanity counts.

Q3. Answer: A-4, B-5, C-3, D-2, E-1

Christian Bale's Patrick Bateman is an investment banker by day, psycho killer by night. Jodie Foster's Clarice Starling hunts Buffalo Bill. Samuel L. Jackson's Jules Winnfield quotes scripture before executing people. Woody comes alive when Andy leaves the room. Keanu Reeves' Neo was so dedicated he learned all the complex fight choreography himself, even after undergoing neck surgery just before filming began.

Q4. Answer: A-4, B-3, C-6, D-2, E-1, F-5

Tarantino revolutionized indie film with non-linear storytelling. The giant outdoor water tank built for Titanic's exterior scenes in Mexico held 17 million gallons of water and had its own dedicated ocean horizon, making it the largest filming tank in the world at the time. Shyamalan's twist endings started with The Sixth Sense. Spielberg proved he could do serious drama. The Wachowskis bent reality. Fincher made everyone question consumerism.

Q5. Answer: A) The Bodyguard

Whitney Houston's soundtrack sold over 45 million copies worldwide, making it the best-selling soundtrack ever. Kevin Costner suggested covering "I Will Always Love You" and proposed the iconic a cappella opening. The film was mediocre, but Houston's voice carried it to massive success.

Q6. Answer: A-5, B-2, C-4, D-1, E-3

Tom Hanks made Forrest Gump lovable and won his second consecutive Oscar. Edward Norton and Brad Pitt took a brief soap-making course before filming Fight Club to convincingly portray their characters' side hustle. Some of the soap they made actually appeared on screen. Jim Carrey showed dramatic range in The Truman Show. Robin Williams proved he could do drama in Good Will Hunting. Samuel L. Jackson made Jules terrifying and philosophical.

Q7. Answer: A-4, B-1, C-2, D-5, E-3

Val Kilmer voiced Moses and God in The Prince of Egypt. To avoid controversy, all major actors whispered God's lines so no one voice would dominate. By the time Kilmer read his lines, filmmakers realized they needed someone louder, but you can still hear the rest whispering beneath his voice. Robin Williams improvised so much Genie material (recording hours of extra lines) that filmmakers couldn't submit Aladdin for Best Adapted Screenplay because so much final dialogue was never written in the script. Tom Hanks made Woody iconic. Eddie Murphy's Donkey became Shrek's breakout character. James Earl Jones brought gravitas to Mufasa.

Q8. Answer: A) Ray Liotta in Goodfellas

Ray Liotta's Henry Hill opens with this iconic narration over a freeze frame. The famous long Steadicam shot where Henry and Karen walk through the Copacabana nightclub and kitchen was only rehearsed twice before Scorsese decided to film it. It was completed in one single, iconic take. Liotta's voiceover carries the film, making you sympathize with criminals doing terrible things. The film became the definitive mob movie of the 90s.

Q9. Answer: A-4, B-2, C-5, D-3, E-1

The Pixies' "Where Is My Mind?" wasn't written for Fight Club but became inseparable from its ending. David Fincher chose it to underscore the destruction of credit card company buildings as the ultimate anti-consumerist statement. The song's dreamy, detached quality perfectly matched the surreal chaos on screen. Brad Pitt and Edward Norton actually learned to make soap, taking a brief course before filming. Some of the soap they made appeared on screen.

Toy Story's animators couldn't render realistic fabric, so they dressed characters in wrinkle-resistant materials. Woody's signature checkered shirt is digitally simulated vinyl. Celine Dion didn't want to record "My Heart Will Go On" initially, but Kevin Costner (who wasn't even in Titanic) had suggested the song and pushed for the a cappella opening. It won an Oscar and dominated radio. "Iris" stayed on charts for months and became Goo Goo Dolls' signature. Seal's "Kiss from a Rose" won three Grammys and outlasted Batman Forever's cultural relevance.

Q10. Answer: Forrest Gump

Tom Hanks played Forrest, who stumbled through major historical events while remaining oblivious to their significance. The famous ping-pong scenes were entirely faked. Hanks never actually hit the ball; the sound effects and ball's movement were all added digitally in post-production. Hanks was just instructed to wave the paddle in the general direction of the non-existent ball. His best friend Bubba was obsessed with shrimp boats. The "box of chocolates" line became one of the most quoted movie lines of the 90s.

Round 8 – Quick Quips

Two small answers, one bigger phrase. Simple in theory, trickier in practice.

Example

Clue A: Underground passage → Tunnel
Clue B: Intense focus → Vision
Combined Answer: Tunnel Vision

Q1

Clue A: Low temperature →
Clue B: Joint between neck and arm →

Q2

Clue A: Act of slicing →
Clue B: Border of a blade →

Q3

Clue A: Unable to see →
Clue B: Small area or mark →

Q4

Clue A: Comedic payoff to a joke →
Clue B: Row of words →

Q5

Clue A: Opposite of coarse →
Clue B: Text on paper →

Q6

Clue A: Not tight →
Clue B: Shipboard artillery →

Q7

Clue A: Four-sided shape →
Clue B: First whole number →

Q8

Clue A: High temperature →
Clue B: One of the most important food crops, cooked and eaten as a
vegetable →

Q9

Clue A: Opposite of late →
Clue B: Proverbial worm seeker →

Q10

Clue A: Opposite of small →
Clue B: A complete or overall view →

Round 8 Answers

Punch lines delivered, time to see if your phrases landed or flopped.

Q1. Answer: Cold Shoulder

When you give someone the cold shoulder, you're deliberately ignoring them or being unfriendly. The "cold shoulder of mutton" story is actually folk etymology (a made-up origin that sounds good but isn't true). The phrase probably comes from a mistranslation of a Vulgate Bible phrase meaning "to turn one's back." Its first recorded use was by Sir Walter Scott in 1816.

Q2. Answer: Cutting Edge

Something cutting edge is at the forefront of innovation or technology. Originally a literal term for the sharpest part of a blade, it evolved to describe anything pioneering or state-of-the-art.

Q3. Answer: Blind Spot

Your blind spot is something you can't see or don't notice, whether literally (like the area your car mirrors don't cover) or figuratively (like a personal weakness you're unaware of). Everyone has them, which is why they're so dangerous.

Q4. Answer: Punch Line

The final part of a joke that makes it funny. The term comes from the idea that a good ending "punches" you with surprise or laughter. Without a strong punch line, even a well-set-up joke falls flat.

Q5. Answer: Fine Print

The small, often overlooked text in contracts or agreements where important details hide. It's called "fine" because the text is literally smaller and finer than the main text. Always read it, especially before signing anything.

Q6. Answer: Loose Cannon

Someone unpredictable or hard to control. The phrase comes from naval warfare, when a cannon that broke free from its moorings would roll dangerously around the deck, crushing anything in its path. A literal disaster waiting to happen.

Q7. Answer: Square One

Going back to square one means starting over from the beginning. The origin is debated between two theories: board games where you literally return to the first square, or early 20th-century radio commentators who used a numbered grid system to describe football (soccer) matches to listeners who couldn't see the field.

Q8. Answer: Hot Potato

A controversial issue that people want to pass off quickly to avoid dealing with. Like an actual hot potato fresh from the oven, you don't want to hold onto it for long because it's uncomfortable or risky.

Q9. Answer: Early Bird

The early bird gets the worm, as the saying goes. Someone who's an early bird wakes up or arrives before others, usually gaining an advantage. Morning people love this phrase. Night owls are less convinced.

Q10. Answer: Big Picture

The overall situation or long-term perspective, as opposed to small details. When someone tells you to look at the big picture, they're asking you to step back and see how everything connects rather than getting lost in specifics.

Round 9 – School Days: STEM Edition

Remember cramming for science and math tests back in school? Now you're 50, and the only formula you use daily is how much coffee it takes to function. Let's see what stuck besides the memory of squeaky chalk.

Q1. DNA Basics

What does the N stand for in DNA?

A) Nitrogen
B) Nucleic
C) Neutron
D) Nucleus

Q2. Human Anatomy

Which part of the human eye controls the amount of light that enters?

A) Retina
B) Iris
C) Cornea
D) Lens

Q3. Chemical Symbols Match

Match each element symbol (A-D) with the element name (1-4):

Symbols:

A) W
B) Au
C) O
D) Ag

Elements:

1. Oxygen
2. Silver
3. Gold
4. Tungsten

Q4. Physics Formula

According to Newton's Second Law, force equals what?

A) Work × Distance
B) Mass ÷ Velocity
C) Energy ÷ Time
D) Mass × Acceleration

Q5. Math Problems

A) Which of the following equals 81? (2^4, 3^4, 4^3, 9^3)
B) If a rectangle has length 12 cm and width 7 cm, what is its area?
C) What is 15% of 200?

Q6. Probability Problem

You flip a fair coin twice. What is the probability of getting two heads?

A) 1/2
B) 1/3
C) 1/4
D) 1/6

Q7. Equation ID

The equation $E = mc^2$ relates energy, mass, and the speed of light. Which scientist is famous for this equation?

A) Isaac Newton
B) Albert Einstein
C) Stephen Hawking
D) Niels Bohr

Q8. Inventor Match

Match each inventor/scientist (A-E) with their invention/discovery (1-5):

Inventors:

A) Alexander Graham Bell
B) Alexander Fleming

C) Thomas Edison
D) J. Robert Oppenheimer
E) Marie Curie

Inventions/Discoveries:

1. Radioactivity research and isolation of radium and polonium
2. Penicillin antibiotic
3. Led the development of the atomic bomb
4. Practical incandescent light bulb
5. Telephone communication device

Q9. True or False

A) An obtuse angle is smaller than 90°
B) URL stands for Uniform Resource Locator
C) The human body has 206 bones
D) Water boils at 100°C at all altitudes

Q10. Solar System Order

Arrange these planets in order from closest to farthest from the Sun:

A) Mars, Venus, Earth, Mercury
B) Mercury, Venus, Earth, Mars
C) Venus, Mercury, Mars, Earth
D) Mercury, Earth, Venus, Mars

Did You Know? History at 45 RPM

Billy Joel's rapid-fire hit "We Didn't Start the Fire" is basically a history quiz set to music. Released in 1989, as Joel turned 40, the song crams 119 distinct historical references into a catchy 4½-minute package. Starting with Harry Truman in 1949 and ending with "Rock & Roller Cola Wars" in 1989, Joel reels off events, people, and pop culture from the Cold War era in breathless succession.

The song emerged from a specific generational argument. A 21-year-old friend complained to Joel about how terrible the world was in the 1980s, prompting the musician to counter that every generation faces similar challenges. Joel began listing historical events from his own youth to prove his point, and that impromptu history lesson became the blueprint for what would become one of his biggest hits. Sound familiar? If you're celebrating your 60th birthday in 2025, you've probably had this exact conversation from both sides. You've listened to younger people complain about today's problems while thinking about the challenges you faced growing up in the 1970s and 80s. You've also likely caught yourself romanticizing "simpler times" when talking to people older than yourself, conveniently forgetting about oil crises, Cold War tensions, and Watergate scandals that shaped your youth.

Ironically, Joel himself has never been particularly fond of his creation, dismissing it as a "novelty song" and comparing its melody to "a dentist's drill." The artist's ambivalence toward his own work adds an unexpected layer to a song that millions found both catchy and educational.

The Ultimate Name-Drop

In verses that don't even bother to rhyme properly, Joel rattles through everything from Sputnik and Chubby Checker to Belgians in the Congo, the Vietnam War, Woodstock, Watergate, and dozens more. Each line functions as a headline from its time, creating a dizzying montage of four decades. The song reads like someone's particularly well-informed stream of consciousness, jumping from Joseph Stalin to Marilyn Monroe to the Bay of Pigs without pausing for breath.

Joel wrote the song after a younger friend complained that the 1980s were a "terrible time" to be young. Joel's response was essentially, "Hold my beer," as he proceeded to chronicle forty years of nonstop turmoil to prove that every generation inherits chaos. The resulting track became an accidental masterpiece of compression, fitting nearly half a century of major events into the time it takes most songs to establish a mood.

Educational Phenomenon

Teachers embraced the song as a classroom tool, using it to spark student interest in post-World War II history. Suddenly, memorizing historical events became a musical challenge rather than academic drudgery. Students found themselves accidentally learning about the Korean War, McCarthyism, and the Space Race while trying to master Joel's tongue-twisting delivery. The song proved that education could be entertaining, though it probably gave social studies teachers headaches trying to explain why "Trouble in the Suez" appeared in the same verse as "Little Rock."

Educators developed sophisticated lesson plans around the track's 119 references. The popular "jigsaw" method divided students into groups, with each team researching specific verses and becoming experts on their assigned historical period before teaching other groups. One high school teacher created an entire semester project requiring students to research every single reference and construct a detailed timeline of post-war America. The approach transformed passive listening into active historical investigation.

The most engaging extension involved students creating their own sequel verses covering events from 1989 onward. These assignments required research skills while letting students exercise creativity, demonstrating that history continues beyond textbook chapters. Students suddenly grasped that major events were still unfolding around them, not just frozen in dusty archives. The exercise proved particularly powerful for helping teenagers understand that they were living through history rather than simply studying it.

The track's educational value extended beyond formal classrooms. For anyone who grew up hearing it on the radio, the song served as an inadvertent crash course in Cold War history. References that seemed meaningless to young listeners gradually gained significance as they encountered the actual events in school or through life experience. "We Didn't Start the Fire" became a generational Rosetta Stone, helping decode the historical anxieties that shaped their parents' worldview.

The Boomer Defense

The chorus delivers the song's central message with deceptive simplicity. "We didn't start the fire, it was always burning since the world's been turning" functions as both historical observation and generational defense. Joel was essentially arguing that Baby Boomers shouldn't be blamed for the world's problems since they inherited most of them from previous generations. This perspective resonated during an era when younger people were criticizing Boomer policies and cultural choices.

The song's structure reinforces this argument by demonstrating how quickly world events pile up. Each decade brings its own crises, scandals, and cultural shifts, suggesting that chaos is humanity's natural state rather than the product of any single generation's failures. By the time Joel reaches the song's end in 1989, the accumulation of references creates an almost overwhelming sense of historical momentum.

The music video amplified this effect through visual storytelling. It followed a married couple and their children from 1949 to 1989, showing their house and clothing evolving to reflect each era's distinct style and cultural markers. As the song's historical references flew by, viewers watched the family age against backdrops of changing decor, fashion, and technology. The video reinforced Joel's central argument by making the passage of time viscerally apparent, showing how quickly decades compress into memory while the chaos of each moment felt overwhelming to those living through it.

Still Burning Bright

Nearly 35 years after its release, "We Didn't Start the Fire" remains culturally relevant in ways Joel probably never anticipated. The song established a template for musical historical commentary that continues to influence artists today. In 2023, Fall Out Boy released an updated version covering events from 1990 to 2023, though they faced criticism for abandoning Joel's chronological structure. The band deliberately placed major events like 9/11 and George Floyd's death in specific positions for emotional impact rather than maintaining strict timeline accuracy.

The original's enduring appeal lies in its reminder that historical perspective requires patience. Events that seem uniquely catastrophic to one generation often represent variations on eternal human themes. Wars, scandals, technological disruptions, and cultural upheavals have always existed; only the specific details change. Joel's rapid-fire delivery mirrors how quickly major events can feel overwhelming when experienced in real-time, yet the song's catchy melody suggests that even chaos can be made bearable through the right artistic treatment.

Joel's breathless recitation of disparate facts proved accidentally prophetic. The song anticipated our current information-saturated age, where news cycles compress decades of change into daily headlines and social media feeds fragment attention across countless simultaneous crises. His format perfectly predicted how people would need to process enormous amounts of historical information at accelerated speeds. The track functions as both artifact of its time and preview of our digital future, where everyone has become their own Billy Joel, frantically cataloging the chaos scrolling past their screens. At 60, you've now experienced both sides of Joel's generational argument: you've lived through the "terrible" times he catalogued, and you're watching new generations discover that the fire never actually went out.

Round 9 Answers

Turns out high school wasn't that long ago... unless you're counting in dog years. Time to grade yourself.

Q1. Answer: B) Nucleic

DNA stands for Deoxyribonucleic Acid. The N is for Nucleic, not Nitrogen. DNA carries genetic instructions in all living things and is shaped like a double helix. Watson and Crick figured out its structure in 1953, though Rosalind Franklin's X-ray work was crucial and often underrecognized.

Q2. Answer: B) Iris

The iris is the colored part of your eye that expands and contracts to control how much light hits the retina, in bright light it constricts the pupil to pinpoint size, while in darkness it dilates wide open. Eye color (blue, brown, green, hazel) is determined by melanin concentration in the iris: more melanin creates brown eyes, while less produces blue or green. The iris contains two sets of muscles working in opposition: the sphincter muscle contracts the pupil, while the dilator muscle expands it.

Interestingly, your iris pattern is completely unique, even more distinctive than fingerprints, which is why iris scanning is used for high-security identification. The iris develops during the first year of life, which is why many babies are born with blue eyes that later change color as melanin production increases.

Q3. Answer: A-4, B-3, C-1, D-2

Tungsten's symbol is W from its German name "Wolfram." It has the highest melting point of all metals and is used in light bulb filaments. Gold is Au from Latin "aurum," doesn't corrode, perfect for jewelry and electronics. Oxygen is O, atomic number 8, essential for breathing. Silver is Ag from Latin "argentum," used in mirrors and photography. The periodic table uses Latin and German names, which is why symbols don't always match English.

Q4. Answer: D) Mass × Acceleration

Newton's Second Law is F = ma. Force equals mass times acceleration. Push a shopping cart (low mass) and it accelerates easily. Push a car (high mass) with the same force and it barely moves. This fundamental physics explains why trucks take longer to stop than cars. Newton figured this out in the 1600s.

Newton was famously terrible at relationships and probably died a virgin. He had a nervous breakdown at 50 and spent years obsessed with alchemy, trying to turn lead into gold. Despite inventing calculus and revolutionizing physics, he wasted decades on biblical prophecy and occult manuscripts. His rival Robert Hooke accused him of stealing ideas, and Newton was so petty he waited until Hooke died before publishing his work on optics.

The apple story is probably true, though. Newton did see an apple fall and wondered why it fell straight down instead of sideways or up. That observation led to universal gravitation. He also invented the cat flap (the little door for cats) because his cat kept interrupting his experiments. Genius at physics, useless at basic human interaction.

Q5. Answer: A) 3^4, B) 84 cm^2, C) 30

The number that equals 81 is 3^4, since $3 \times 3 \times 3 \times 3 = 81$, while $2^4 = 16$, $4^3 = 64$, and $9^3 = 729$. The rectangle's area is $12 \times 7 = 84$ cm^2. Finally, 15% of 200 works out to 30.

Q6. Answer: C) 1/4

Understanding the problem: Two coin flips means we need to consider all possible combinations.

List all possible outcomes: First flip → Second flip = Result Heads → Heads = HH Heads → Tails = HT Tails → Heads = TH Tails → Tails = TT

Total possible outcomes = 4 These outcomes are mutually exclusive (only one can happen at a time)

Count favorable outcomes: We want both heads (HH) Favorable outcomes = 1

Calculate probability: Probability = Favorable outcomes ÷ Total outcomes Probability = 1 ÷ 4 Probability = 1/4 or 25%

Alternative method (multiplication rule): Each flip is independent (the first flip doesn't affect the second) Probability of heads on first flip = 1/2 Probability of heads on second flip = 1/2 Probability of both = 1/2 × 1/2 = 1/4

People often guess 1/2 because they think "heads or tails" but forget to account for all possible combinations across both flips.

Q7. Answer: B) Albert Einstein

Einstein's $E = mc^2$ from his 1905 special relativity paper showed that mass and energy are interchangeable. A tiny amount of mass can become enormous energy because c (speed of light) is huge and you're squaring it. This equation explains nuclear power, atomic bombs, and how the sun works. Probably the most famous equation in physics.

The equation reveals that converting just one kilogram of matter into pure energy would release approximately 90 quadrillion joules, equivalent to the energy of 21 megatons of TNT or roughly 1,500 times the Hiroshima bomb. The sun converts about 4 million tons of mass into energy every second through nuclear fusion, which is why it can shine for billions of years. Einstein published this equation as an afterthought, a three page follow up paper to his special relativity work, with the casual title "Does the Inertia of a Body Depend Upon Its Energy Content?" He had no idea it would become the most recognized formula in science or that it would unlock both the devastating power of nuclear weapons and the potential for clean fusion energy.

Q8. Answer: A-5, B-2, C-4, D-3, E-1

Bell patented the telephone in 1876, though the invention's credit is contested with Elisha Gray and Antonio Meucci. Fleming discovered penicillin by accident in 1928 when mold killed bacteria in his petri dishes. His messy lab habits led to the discovery that saved millions of lives. Edison didn't invent the light bulb but made the first practical one in 1879 that could last long enough to be commercially useful.

Oppenheimer led the Manhattan Project, developing the atomic bomb during World War II. After seeing its destruction, he famously quoted the Bhagavad Gita: "Now I am become Death, the destroyer of worlds." Marie Curie was the first woman to win a Nobel Prize and the only person to win Nobel Prizes in two different sciences (Physics and Chemistry). Her research on radioactivity killed her, she died from radiation exposure in 1934.

Q9. Answer: A) FALSE, B) TRUE, C) TRUE, D) FALSE

An obtuse angle is greater than 90° but less than 180°. Acute angles are smaller than 90°. Easy to mix up if you haven't thought about it since school. URL does stand for Uniform Resource Locator, how web browsers find websites. Tim Berners-Lee invented URLs in 1994 as part of creating the World Wide Web.

The human body has 206 bones in adults. Babies are born with about 270 bones, but many fuse together as they grow. Water boils at 100°C (212°F) only at sea level. At higher altitudes, atmospheric pressure is lower, so water boils at lower temperatures. On Mount Everest, water boils at about 70°C. This is why cooking takes longer in the mountains and why pressure cookers exist.

Q10. Answer: B) Mercury, Venus, Earth, Mars

The inner four rocky planets in order from the Sun are Mercury, Venus, Earth, and Mars. Easy mnemonic: "My Very Educated Mother" (for the full solar system it continues "Just Served Us Nachos" for Jupiter, Saturn, Uranus, Neptune). Pluto used to be ninth but got demoted to dwarf planet in 2006 after astronomers discovered similar sized objects in the Kuiper Belt, forcing a redefinition of what constitutes a planet.

Mercury is closest to the Sun, scorching hot on the sunny side (800°F) but freezing in shadow (290°F below zero) because it has almost no atmosphere to distribute heat. A day on Mercury (one full rotation) takes 59 Earth days, but a year (one orbit around the Sun) only takes 88 Earth days, meaning a Mercury day is longer than its year. Venus is actually the hottest planet despite being second from the Sun because its thick carbon dioxide atmosphere traps heat in a runaway greenhouse effect, with surface temperatures reaching 900°F, hot enough to melt lead.

Mars is the fourth planet, the red planet colored by iron oxide (rust) covering its surface. Mars has the largest volcano in the solar system (Olympus Mons, three times the height of Mount Everest) and a canyon system (Valles Marineris) that would stretch across the entire United States. Evidence suggests Mars once had liquid water and a thicker atmosphere, making it the prime candidate for finding past microbial life and the focus of future human colonization efforts.

Round 10 – World Stage

Geography is one thing, but this round leans political, capitals, leaders, and the kind of summit headlines that shape history. Consider it your crash course in foreign affairs

Q1. Capital Challenge

Match each country with its capital city:

A) Kazakhstan
B) Myanmar
C) Sri Lanka
D) Benin

Capital Cities:

1. Naypyidaw
2. Sri Jayawardenepura Kotte
3. Astana
4. Porto-Novo

Q2. Summit Stories

In 1982, which country invaded the Falkland Islands, sparking a 10-week war with the United Kingdom?

A) Chile
B) Argentina
C) Brazil
D) Uruguay

Q3. Leaders and Countries

Match each leader (A-H) with their country (1-8):

Leaders:

A) Gordon Brown
B) Gerhard Schröder
C) Lula da Silva

D) Benazir Bhutto
E) Lee Kuan Yew
F) Kim Dae-jung
G) Jacques Chirac
H) Junichiro Koizumi

Countries:

1. Singapore
2. Pakistan
3. United Kingdom
4. Germany
5. Brazil
6. South Korea
7. Japan
8. France

Q4. Map Mismatch

Which country does NOT border the Caspian Sea?

A) Kazakhstan
B) Turkmenistan
C) Azerbaijan
D) Uzbekistan

Q5. Coup or No Coup? True or False

A) Laos's Pol Pot seized power through a military coup in 1975

B) Chile's Augusto Pinochet overthrew Salvador Allende in a 1973 coup and was later arrested in London in 1998

C) Iran's Ayatollah Khomeini took control through a military coup backed by the Revolutionary Guard

D) Pakistan's Pervez Musharraf overthrew Prime Minister Benazir Bhutto in a coup in 1999

Q6. Cold War Conflicts

Which country did the Soviet Union invade in 1979, sparking a decade-long war that became known as "the Soviet Vietnam"?

A) Iran
B) Afghanistan
C) Pakistan
D) Turkey

Q7. Map Mismatch

Which country does NOT border the Mediterranean Sea?

A) Albania
B) Croatia
C) Montenegro
D) Bulgaria

Q8. Who Am I?

I ruled Libya for 42 years after seizing power in a 1969 coup at age 27. I lived in a tent, had an all-female bodyguard squad, and wrote the Green Book outlining my political philosophy. I was killed during the 2011 Arab Spring uprising. Who am I?

Q9. Summit Stories

In 1978, this U.S. president brokered peace between Egypt and Israel at Camp David. Egyptian President Anwar Sadat and Israeli Prime Minister Menachem Begin signed the accords, leading to the first peace treaty between Israel and an Arab nation. Who was the U.S. president?

Q10. Map Mismatch

Which country does NOT border the Baltic Sea?

A) Sweden
B) Finland
C) Lithuania
D) Belarus

Round 10 Answers

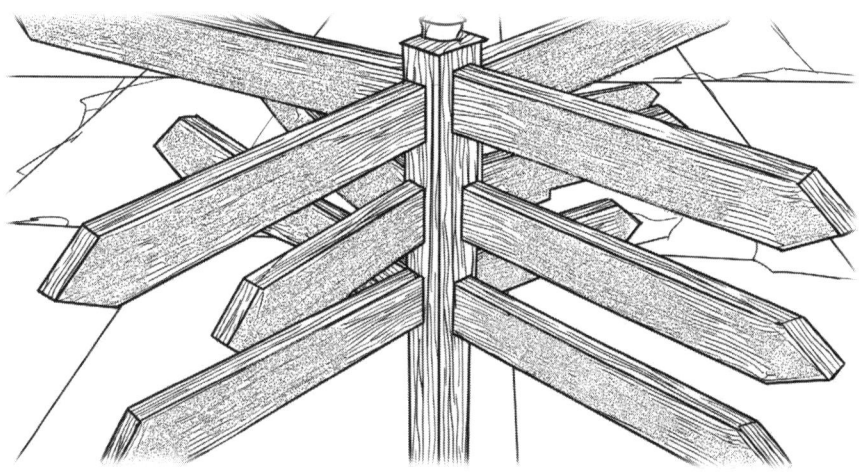

Like election night tallies, the numbers don't lie. Time to see where you stand on the world stage.

Q1. Answer: A-3, B-1, C-2, D-4

Kazakhstan couldn't decide on a capital name. Almaty to Astana in 1997, then Nur-Sultan in 2019 (after their dictator president), then back to Astana in 2022 when even they got embarrassed. Myanmar's generals moved the capital to Naypyidaw in 2006, a ghost city built in the jungle where nobody lives. Paranoid military types love building capitals in the middle of nowhere. Sri Lanka's actual capital is Sri Jayawardenepura Kotte, which sounds like someone keyboard-smashed and kept it. Everyone just says Colombo. Benin's capital Porto-Novo gets completely ignored because Cotonou is where everything actually happens, classic case of capital in name only.

Q2. Answer: B) Argentina

Argentina's military junta invaded the Falklands on April 2, 1982, thinking Britain wouldn't sail 8,000 miles to defend some sheep-covered rocks. Bad calculation. Thatcher sent a naval task force, and Britain retook the islands in 74 days. The war killed 649 Argentines and 255 Brits over islands with more penguins than people. Argentina still calls them Las Malvinas and teaches kids they're Argentine territory. The humiliating defeat destroyed Argentina's military dictatorship, which collapsed the next year. One upside to losing a pointless war.

Q3. Answer: A-3, B-4, C-5, D-2, E-1, F-6, G-8, H-7

Brown took over from Blair in 2007 right as the global economy imploded. Fantastic timing. Schröder ran Germany from 1998 to 2005, pushed labor reforms everyone hated, then immediately took a cushy job with Russian gas company Gazprom. Classy. Lula lifted 20 million Brazilians out of poverty, got thrown in prison for corruption, conviction got annulled, then won the presidency again in 2022 at age 77. Wild ride.

Bhutto became Pakistan's first female PM in 1988, got ousted twice for corruption, came back for another try, and was assassinated at a campaign rally in 2007. Lee Kuan Yew turned Singapore from a malarial swamp into Asia's richest city through authoritarian efficiency and banning chewing gum. Kim Dae-jung survived multiple assassination attempts, won a Nobel Prize for his North Korea policy, then watched it completely fail. Koizumi was Japan's Elvis-loving PM who kept visiting the war shrine that pissed off China and Korea. Chirac ran France for 12 years, opposed Iraq War, got convicted of corruption after leaving office.

Q4. Answer: D) Uzbekistan

Uzbekistan is doubly landlocked (only two countries are: Uzbekistan and Liechtenstein). It's surrounded by other landlocked countries. Used to touch the Aral Sea until Soviet cotton farming drained it to 10% of original size, creating one of history's worst ecological disasters. Now there are rusted fishing boats sitting in a desert. The Caspian Sea touches Russia, Kazakhstan, Turkmenistan, Iran, and Azerbaijan. Despite being called a sea, it's actually the world's largest lake with no ocean connection. Salty but not ocean-salty.

Q5. Answer: A) FALSE, B) TRUE, C) FALSE, D) FALSE

Pol Pot was Cambodian, not Laotian. He led the Khmer Rouge in Cambodia, not Laos. The Pathet Lao controlled Laos. Pol Pot's Khmer Rouge won a civil war in 1975, marching into Phnom Penh as the government collapsed. They evacuated the entire city, killed anyone wearing glasses (intellectuals were suspect), and murdered 1.7 million Cambodians before Vietnam invaded in 1979.

Pinochet overthrew democratically elected socialist Salvador Allende on September 11, 1973, with CIA backing. Allende died during the palace attack. Pinochet ruled until 1990, then got arrested in London in 1998 on a Spanish warrant for human rights violations. He was released on medical grounds and died in Chile in 2006.

Khomeini returned from exile during the 1979 Iranian Revolution, a popular uprising with millions in the streets, not a military coup. The Shah fled, Khomeini established an Islamic Republic. Musharraf overthrew Prime Minister Nawaz Sharif (not Benazir Bhutto) in October 1999 after Sharif tried to fire him as army chief. Bhutto was assassinated in 2007.

Q6. Answer: B) Afghanistan

Soviets rolled into Afghanistan on Christmas Eve 1979 to save a communist government. Stayed nine years, lost 15,000 troops, killed over a million Afghans, and achieved absolutely nothing. The U.S. armed the mujahideen rebels with Stinger missiles that could blow Soviet helicopters out of the sky. One of those rebels was Osama bin Laden, which worked out great for everyone later. The war bankrupted the USSR and destroyed morale, contributing to the Soviet collapse in 1991. Then the U.S. invaded Afghanistan in 2001 and stayed 20 years, proving nobody learns anything.

Q7. Answer: D) Bulgaria

Bulgaria's on the Black Sea, not the Med. Albania, Croatia, and Montenegro all have Adriatic coastlines, which is part of the Mediterranean. During the Cold War, Bulgaria's Black Sea coast was where Soviets went on vacation because they couldn't leave the Eastern Bloc. The Black Sea connects to the Mediterranean through Turkey's Bosphorus strait. Name possibly comes from its dark depths or Ottoman directional terminology (black meant north). Either way, less fun than the Mediterranean.

Q8. Answer: Muammar Gaddafi

Gaddafi seized power in 1969 at 27 and ruled for 42 years. Called himself "Brother Leader" and "King of Kings of Africa," lived in a Bedouin tent even when visiting foreign countries (he'd pitch it on their lawn), and kept an all-female bodyguard unit called the Amazonian Guard. His Green Book was political fan fiction mixing socialism, Islam, and Arab nationalism. Sponsored terrorism throughout the 1980s including the Lockerbie bombing. When the Arab Spring hit Libya in 2011, NATO backed the rebels. They found him hiding in a drainage pipe in Sirte, dragged him out, and killed him. Cell phone footage showed him bloodied and begging. Not the dignified exit he probably imagined.

Q9. Answer: Jimmy Carter

Carter locked Sadat and Begin at Camp David for 13 days in September 1978 until they hammered out peace accords. Both leaders won the Nobel Peace Prize (Carter got his later for other stuff). Egypt got back the Sinai Peninsula that Israel grabbed in 1967. Sadat was assassinated three years later by Egyptian military officers who thought making peace with Israel was treason. The treaty held anyway, still the only lasting Arab-Israeli peace deal. Sometimes diplomacy actually works.

Q10. Answer: D) Belarus

Belarus is landlocked. The other three all touch the Baltic Sea along with Estonia, Latvia, Poland, Germany, Denmark, and Russia. The Baltic is one of the least salty seas because rivers constantly dump fresh water into it. Freezes solid in harsh winters.

During the Cold War, it was basically a Soviet lake except for Sweden and Finland's coasts, giving the USSR easy naval access to the North Sea if they needed it.or murder, still debated). Pinochet ruled until 1990, tossing dissidents out of helicopters. Musharraf overthrew Pakistan's Prime Minister Nawaz Sharif in October 1999 after Sharif tried to fire him as army chief. Classic coup. Musharraf ruled until 2008, survived multiple assassination attempts, then fled to avoid treason charges.

Round 11 – Timeline Tangle

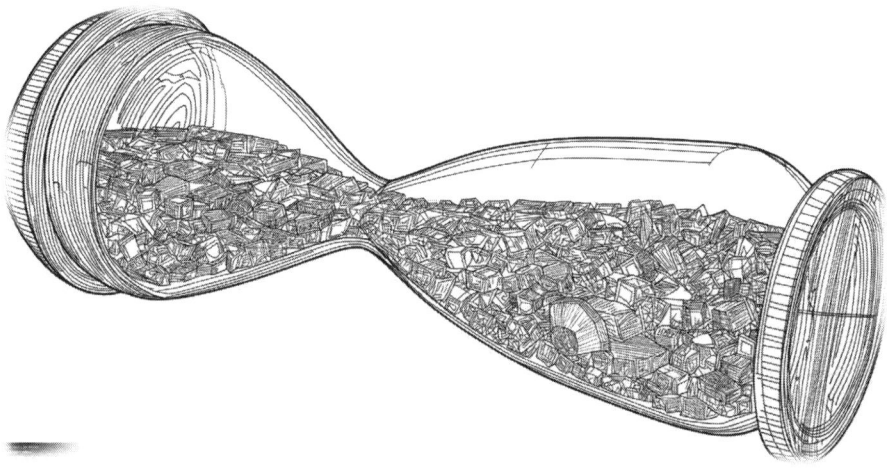

Events thrown in a blender. Your job? Put them back in chronological order.

Questions

Q1. Vietnam War Timeline

Fall of Saigon, Death of Ho Chi Minh, Japan occupies Vietnam, The Tet Offensive, Geneva Accords, JFK escalates U.S. involvement, French defeated at Dien Bien Phu.

Q2. Music's Crazy Moments

Oasis at Knebworth, Nirvana plays MTV Unplugged, Madonna kisses Britney Spears at VMAs, Beatles rooftop concert, Bob Dylan goes electric at Newport Folk Festival, Michael Jackson's hair catches fire, Kanye West interrupts Taylor Swift.

Q3. Sports Shocks

Leicester City win the Premier League, Zidane's World Cup headbutt, Tyson bites Holyfield's ear, Maradona's "Hand of God," Tonya Harding scandal, Super Bowl blackout, Michael Jordan retires (first time), Red Sox break the Curse, Cubs win the World Series.

Q4. TV Milestones

Final episode of Game of Thrones, First episode of The Simpsons, O.J. Simpson car chase, MAS*H finale, Sopranos finale, Netflix launches streaming, First episode of Friends, First episode of I Love Lucy, First episode of The X-Files, First episode of Seinfeld.

Q5. Royal Headlines

Wedding of William and Kate, Queen Elizabeth II's death, Queen Elizabeth II's Golden Jubilee, Wedding of Charles and Diana, Death of Princess Diana, Coronation of Charles III, Harry and Meghan step back from royal duties.

Q6. Disaster Headlines

Indian Ocean tsunami, Fukushima nuclear disaster, Haiti earthquake, Challenger explosion, Chernobyl disaster, 9/11 attacks, Hurricane Katrina, Lockerbie bombing, Mount St. Helens eruption.

Q7. Theme Park Openings

Universal Studios Florida, Shanghai Disneyland, Disney World Florida, Disneyland Paris, Disneyland California, Hong Kong Disneyland, Epcot opens at Disney World.

Q8. Book Releases

Harry Potter and the Philosopher's Stone, The Hunger Games, The Shining, The Da Vinci Code, The Handmaid's Tale, Fifty Shades of Grey, A Game of Thrones, Lord of the Flies.

Q9. Presidential Scandals

Iran-Contra affair, Lewinsky scandal, Watergate scandal, Teapot Dome scandal, Hillary Clinton email controversy, Bill Clinton impeachment, Bush v. Gore Florida recount.

Q10. War on Terror Timeline

Rise of ISIS, U.S. invasion of Iraq, Death of Osama bin Laden, U.S. invasion of Afghanistan, U.S. withdrawal from Afghanistan, 7/7 London bombings, Madrid train bombings, Boston Marathon bombing, Charlie Hebdo attack.

Did You Know? The Yellow Revolution

In December 1989, a quirky animated sitcom about a dysfunctional yellow family debuted and television hasn't been the same since. The Simpsons quickly evolved from simple cartoon shorts on The Tracy Ullman Show into a cultural juggernaut that would redefine what animated television could accomplish. What started as crude sketches became the longest-running American sitcom ever, with over 790 episodes and counting, proving that sometimes the most subversive ideas come disguised as harmless entertainment.

Matt Groening arrived at this moment through an unlikely path. For over a decade, he had been drawing "Life in Hell," an underground comic strip featuring Binky, a neurotic rabbit navigating modern existence with cynical observations about work, relationships, and mortality. The strip ran in alternative weeklies across the country, building Groening a cult following among readers who appreciated its dark wit and anti-establishment attitude. When producer James L. Brooks approached him about creating animated segments for The Tracy Ullman Show, Groening faced a crucial decision: sign away the rights to his beloved rabbit characters, or quickly invent something entirely new.

Sitting in Brooks' office lobby, Groening sketched out a nuclear family in mere minutes, naming them after his own relatives while keeping Bart as an anagram of "brat" for himself. The distinctive yellow skin wasn't accidental but calculated, what Groening later described as "the color of a primal scream" designed to stop channel surfers in their tracks. He placed this fictional family in Springfield, a name borrowed from Springfield, Oregon, near his Portland hometown, but deliberately kept the location ambiguous so the show could belong to anywhere in America. The hasty creation process meant these characters carried none of the legal baggage of "Life in Hell," but all of Groening's satirical DNA remained intact, ready to infect prime-time television with the same irreverent spirit that had made a rabbit's existential crisis surprisingly popular in coffee shops and record stores across the country.

Multi-Generational Viewing

The series created appointment television for an unprecedented demographic: entire families watching together while laughing at completely different jokes. Children enjoyed Bart's pranks and Homer's slapstick mishaps, while parents appreciated sophisticated cultural references and biting social commentary.

This multi-layered approach revolutionized television, demonstrating that animated programming didn't need to choose between intelligence and entertainment. The show's writers crafted episodes that functioned simultaneously as children's cartoons and adult satire, a technique that would influence countless programs afterward.

Cultural Prophecy Machine

The show's writers developed an uncanny ability to predict future events, though the reality was more statistical than supernatural. With hundreds of episodes making thousands of cultural observations over three decades, some educated guesses were bound to prove accurate. The show anticipated smartwatches (1995), video calling (1995), Disney buying 20th Century Fox (1998), Donald Trump's presidency (2000), autocorrect fails (2007), Lady Gaga performing with Tony Bennett (2012), and even specific details like Greece's debt crisis (2001) and the NSA surveillance scandal (2007).

The "predictions" spawned internet conspiracy theories about the show's supposed clairvoyance, but writers simply extrapolated current trends to logical extremes. When you satirize everything for thirty-plus years, occasionally your jokes become tomorrow's headlines. The show's longevity created a statistical inevitability that satirical exaggerations would eventually become literal reality, making The Simpsons less a crystal ball than a very persistent cultural observer with a knack for spotting patterns before everyone else.

Homer's frustrated exclamation "D'oh!" became so universally recognized that the Oxford English Dictionary officially added it in 2001, marking perhaps the first time a grunt of animated frustration achieved legitimate linguistic status. The inclusion represented more than cultural recognition; it acknowledged that The Simpsons had fundamentally altered how Americans expressed disappointment. Children who grew up with Homer's catchphrase carried it into adulthood, making "D'oh!" a generational marker as distinctive as any historical event.

Breaking Animation Barriers

Prior to The Simpsons, animated television was confined to Saturday morning children's programming and simple moral lessons. The show's prime-time success demolished these limitations, proving animation could address complex social issues, political satire, and adult relationships without sacrificing humor or accessibility.

This breakthrough opened doors for every adult animated series that followed, from South Park's anarchic provocation to Family Guy's pop culture obsession. The series collected 37 Emmy nominations and 10 wins, with Time magazine declaring it the best television series of the 20th century. These honors validated animation as a legitimate artistic medium capable of serious cultural commentary. The show's influence spread beyond entertainment into academia, where professors began analyzing episodes as social documents reflecting American anxieties about family, work, religion, and community.

Round 11 Answers

Get these in the right order and you're a historian. Get them wrong and you're just guessing with confidence.

Q1. Answer: Japan occupies Vietnam → French defeated at Dien Bien Phu → Geneva Accords → JFK escalates U.S. involvement → The Tet Offensive → Death of Ho Chi Minh → Fall of Saigon

Japan occupied Vietnam during WWII starting 1940. France got crushed at Dien Bien Phu in 1954 after a 57-day siege, ending their colonial dreams. Geneva Accords split Vietnam at the 17th parallel same year. JFK ramped up military advisors 1961-1963. The Tet Offensive in January 1968 shocked America with coordinated attacks across South Vietnam during a holiday ceasefire. Ho Chi Minh died September 1969 but the war dragged on six more years. Saigon fell April 30, 1975, with helicopters evacuating from rooftops in iconic footage.

Q2. Answer: Bob Dylan goes electric at Newport Folk Festival → Beatles rooftop concert → Michael Jackson's hair catches fire → Nirvana plays MTV Unplugged → Oasis at Knebworth → Madonna kisses Britney Spears at VMAs → Kanye West interrupts Taylor Swift

Dylan went electric July 1965 and folk legend Pete Seeger allegedly grabbed an axe threatening to cut the power cables, shouting about the distorted sound quality ruining the performance. The Beatles played their last public show on a London rooftop January 1969 wearing their wives' coats to stay warm. Ringo wore Maureen's red raincoat, John wore Yoko's fur coat. Police shut it down, perfect chaotic ending.

Jackson's hair caught fire during a Pepsi commercial in 1984 from a pyrotechnic malfunction, causing second-degree scalp burns. The chronic pain from this injury likely contributed to his later painkiller dependence. Nirvana's MTV Unplugged happened November 1993. Cobain decorated the stage with black candles, stargazer lilies, and a crystal chandelier, telling producers to make it look "exactly like a funeral." They refused to play "Smells Like Teen Spirit."

Oasis played Knebworth August 1996 to 250,000 people over two nights, but 2.5 million applied for tickets (over 4% of the UK population), still the largest ticket demand in UK history. Madonna kissed Britney and Christina at the 2003 VMAs, but the camera cut to Justin Timberlake's shocked face right after the Britney kiss, effectively erasing Christina from cultural memory. Kanye grabbed the mic from Taylor at the 2009 VMAs after drinking Hennessy straight from the bottle on the red carpet. Obama called him a "jackass" off the record that week.

Q3. Answer: Maradona's "Hand of God" → Michael Jordan retires (first time) → Tonya Harding scandal → Tyson bites Holyfield's ear → Zidane's World Cup headbutt → Red Sox break the Curse → Super Bowl blackout → Cubs win the World Series → Leicester City win the Premier League

Maradona punched the ball past England's keeper in the 1986 World Cup, claiming God's hand did it. Jordan retired in 1993 to play baseball (badly). Harding's ex-husband hired someone to club Nancy Kerrigan's knee January 1994. Tyson bit Holyfield's ear twice in June 1997, got disqualified. Zidane headbutted Materazzi in the 2006 World Cup final, red card in his last match. Red Sox won in 2004, ending an 86-year curse. Super Bowl blackout happened 2013, Ravens vs 49ers. Cubs won 2016 after 108 years. Leicester won the Premier League 2016 at 5000-1 odds, greatest underdog story in sports.

Q4. Answer: First episode of I Love Lucy → MAS*H finale → First episode of The Simpsons → First episode of Seinfeld → First episode of The X-Files → First episode of Friends → O.J. Simpson car chase → Netflix launches streaming → Sopranos finale → Final episode of Game of Thrones

I Love Lucy premiered October 1951, revolutionized TV. MAS*H finale aired February 1983 with 105.9 million viewers, still the record. Simpsons premiered December 1989. Seinfeld premiered July 1989 (actually a few months before Simpsons). X-Files premiered September 1993. Friends premiered September 1994. OJ's white Bronco chase happened June 1994, 95 million watched. Netflix launched streaming January 2007. Sopranos finale aired June 2007, cut to black and broke everyone's TV. Game of Thrones finale aired May 2019, disappointed millions.

Q5. Answer: Wedding of Charles and Diana → Death of Princess Diana → Queen Elizabeth II's Golden Jubilee → Wedding of William and Kate → Harry and Meghan step back from royal duties → Queen Elizabeth II's death → Coronation of Charles III

Charles and Diana married July 1981, 750 million watched. Diana died August 1997 in a Paris tunnel. Golden Jubilee celebrated 50 years on throne in 2002. William and Kate married April 2011 at Westminster Abbey. Harry and Meghan quit being working royals January 2020, moved to California. The Queen died September 2022 at 96 after 70 years. Charles got crowned May 2023, waiting his whole life for the job.

Q6. Answer: Mount St. Helens eruption → Challenger explosion → Chernobyl disaster → Lockerbie bombing → 9/11 attacks → Indian Ocean tsunami → Hurricane Katrina → Haiti earthquake → Fukushima nuclear disaster

Mount St. Helens blew May 1980, killed 57 people in Washington. Challenger exploded January 1986 with teacher Christa McAuliffe aboard, watched live by schoolkids everywhere. Chernobyl melted down April 1986, worst nuclear disaster ever. Pan Am 103 exploded over Lockerbie, Scotland December 1988, Libyan terrorists. 9/11 happened September 2001, nearly 3,000 dead. Indian Ocean tsunami December 2004 killed 230,000 across multiple countries. Katrina devastated New Orleans August 2005, killed 1,800. Haiti earthquake January 2010 killed over 200,000. Fukushima melted down March 2011 after an earthquake and tsunami hit Japan.

Q7. Answer: Disneyland California → Disney World Florida → Epcot opens at Disney World → Universal Studios Florida → Disneyland Paris → Hong Kong Disneyland → Shanghai Disneyland

Disneyland opened Anaheim July 1955, Walt's first park. Disney World opened Orlando October 1971. Epcot opened at Disney World October 1982. Universal Studios Florida opened June 1990. Disneyland Paris opened April 1992 as Euro Disney, nearly bankrupted the company with European resistance. Hong Kong Disneyland opened September 2005. Shanghai Disneyland opened June 2016, first park in mainland China.

Q8. Answer: Lord of the Flies → The Shining → The Handmaid's Tale → A Game of Thrones → Harry Potter and the Philosopher's

Stone → The Da Vinci Code → The Hunger Games → Fifty Shades of Grey

Lord of the Flies published 1954 by William Golding. The Shining published 1977 by Stephen King. The Handmaid's Tale published 1985 by Margaret Atwood. A Game of Thrones published 1996 by George R.R. Martin, who still hasn't finished the series 28 years later. Harry Potter published 1997, initial print run of 500 copies, Rowling now richer than the Queen was. The Da Vinci Code published 2003 by Dan Brown. The Hunger Games published 2008 by Suzanne Collins. Fifty Shades of Grey published 2011, started as Twilight fan fiction.

Q9. Answer: Teapot Dome scandal → Watergate scandal → Iran-Contra affair → Lewinsky scandal → Bill Clinton impeachment → Bush v. Gore Florida recount → Hillary Clinton email controversy

Teapot Dome under Harding, early 1920s oil reserve bribes. Watergate 1972-1974, Nixon resigned August 1974. Iran-Contra 1985-1987 under Reagan, secretly selling arms to Iran. Lewinsky scandal broke 1998, Clinton and White House intern. Clinton impeached December 1998, acquitted by Senate. Bush v. Gore Florida recount November-December 2000, Supreme Court decided it. Hillary's email controversy emerged 2015 during her presidential campaign, hurt her badly.

Q10. Answer: U.S. invasion of Afghanistan → U.S. invasion of Iraq → Madrid train bombings → 7/7 London bombings → Death of Osama bin Laden → Boston Marathon bombing → Rise of ISIS → Charlie Hebdo attack → U.S. withdrawal from Afghanistan

U.S. invaded Afghanistan October 2001 after 9/11. Invaded Iraq March 2003 claiming WMDs (found none). Madrid trains bombed March 2004, killed 193. London 7/7 July 2005, killed 52. Bin Laden killed May 2011 in Pakistan by SEAL Team 6. Boston Marathon bombed April 2013, Tsarnaev brothers killed 3. ISIS declared caliphate 2014 across Iraq and Syria. Charlie Hebdo attacked Paris January 2015, killed 12. U.S. withdrew from Afghanistan August 2021, Taliban retook control immediately.

Round 12 – Solo Stars

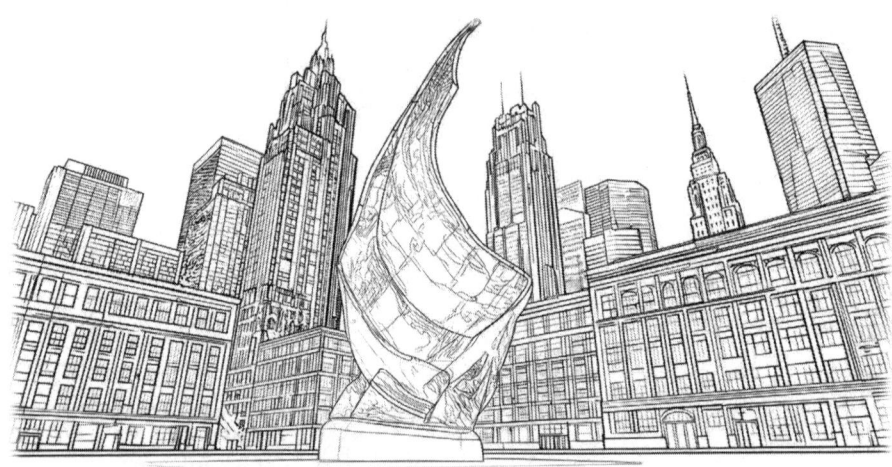

From Motown legends to disco divas, pop icons to hip-hop royalty, these performers didn't need a band to make history.

Q1. Album Match

Match each album (A-H) with the solo artist (1-8):

A) Thriller
B) Purple Rain
C) 21
D) Born to Run
E) Lemonade
F) The Miseducation of Lauryn Hill
G) Tapestry
H) Back to Black

Artists:

1. Beyoncé
2. Bruce Springsteen
3. Prince
4. Adele
5. Michael Jackson
6. Carole King

7. Lauryn Hill
8. Amy Winehouse

Q2. 80s & 90s Solo Hits Timeline

Put these solo artist songs in chronological order by release date:

Billie Jean (Michael Jackson), Like a Prayer (Madonna), Kiss (Prince), ...Baby One More Time (Britney Spears), Genie in a Bottle (Christina Aguilera), Vogue (Madonna), Un-Break My Heart (Toni Braxton), Smooth (Santana feat. Rob Thomas)

Q3. Solo Artist True or False

A) Whitney Houston's "I Will Always Love You" was originally written by Dolly Parton

B) Prince wrote "Nothing Compares 2 U" for Sinéad O'Connor

C) Elton John's "Candle in the Wind 1997" is the best-selling single by a solo artist

D) Madonna was born in Detroit, Michigan

E) Amy Winehouse won five Grammy Awards in one night

F) Justin Timberlake left *NSYNC to join a rock band but quit within a year

Q4. Motown Geography

Which city is known as the birthplace of Motown, launching solo careers of Marvin Gaye, Stevie Wonder, and Diana Ross?

A) Chicago
B) Memphis
C) Atlanta
D) Detroit

Q5. Hip-Hop Geography

Tupac Shakur was fatally shot in 1996 in which city?

A) Los Angeles
B) Las Vegas
C) Compton
D) New York

Q6. Studio 54

Which New York nightclub became the symbol of disco where solo artists like Donna Summer, Diana Ross, and Grace Jones performed?

A) CBGB
B) Studio 54
C) The Apollo Theater
D) Webster Hall

Q7. Rod Stewart Cover Songs

Rod Stewart is known for "Da Ya Think I'm Sexy?" but he also covered many songs. Match each Rod Stewart cover (A-F) with the original artist (1-6):

A) "Maggie May"

B) "The First Cut Is the Deepest"

C) "Downtown Train"

D) "Have I Told You Lately"

E) "Handbags and Gladrags"

F) "Have You Ever Seen the Rain"

Original Artists:

1. Cat Stevens
2. Tom Waits
3. Van Morrison
4. Rod Stewart (original)
5. Creedence Clearwater Revival
6. Chris Farlowe (written by Mike d'Abo)

Q8. Controversial Solo Track

Lou Reed's "Walk on the Wild Side" (1972) referenced drag queens, drugs, and hustlers but made it onto mainstream radio because:

A) Radio censors edited out all controversial lyrics
B) The song was released as an instrumental version for radio
C) Censors didn't understand the slang references
D) RCA Records bribed radio stations to play the unedited version

Q9. Solo Venue Launch Pad

Which Harlem venue's Amateur Night launched careers of Ella Fitzgerald, James Brown, and Lauryn Hill?

A) The Cotton Club
B) The Apollo Theater
C) Blue Note
D) Village Vanguard

Q10. Who Am I?

I was born in Zanzibar but Britain made me a legend. With a four-octave voice, I strutted in a crown and yellow jacket. I wrote of champions and bohemian rhapsodies. My mustache was famous, my moves fearless. Who Am I?

Round 12 Answers

Get these right and you're a music encyclopedia. Get them wrong and you're probably just humming along to Spotify playlists without reading the liner notes.

Q1. Answer: A-5, B-3, C-4, D-2, E-1, F-7, G-6, H-8

Thriller (1982) made Jackson the King of Pop, selling 70 million copies. Purple Rain (1984) was Prince's masterpiece, blending rock, funk, and pop into a soundtrack phenomenon. 21 (2011) made Adele a global superstar, selling 31 million copies with "Rolling in the Deep" and "Someone Like You." Born to Run (1975) turned Springsteen into a rock icon with epic storytelling. Lemonade (2016) was Beyoncé's visual album addressing infidelity and Black identity, winning critical acclaim.

The Miseducation of Lauryn Hill (1998) won five Grammys and blended hip-hop, soul, and reggae into something completely new. She never released another solo album after, making it one of music's greatest one-and-dones. Tapestry (1971) by Carole King spent 15 consecutive weeks at number one, selling 25 million copies. It's one of the best-selling albums by a female artist ever. Back to Black (2006) made Amy Winehouse a star with retro soul production and brutally honest lyrics about addiction and heartbreak. She died in 2011 at 27, joining the cursed club.

Q2. Answer: Billie Jean → Kiss → Like a Prayer → Vogue → Un-Break My Heart → ...Baby One More Time → Genie in a Bottle → Smooth

Jackson's "Billie Jean" (1983) dominated MTV with the moonwalk debut. Prince's "Kiss" (1986) was minimalist funk perfection, stripping everything down to falsetto and rhythm. Madonna's "Like a Prayer" (1989) caused religious controversy with crosses and burning imagery, Pepsi pulled their ad deal. "Vogue" (1990) launched voguing from underground ballrooms to pop radio. Toni Braxton's "Un-Break My Heart" (1996) spent 11 weeks at number one, becoming one of the biggest ballads of the 90s. Britney's "...Baby One More Time" (1998) launched teen pop's comeback. Christina's "Genie in a Bottle" (1999) followed months later. Santana's "Smooth" with Rob Thomas (1999) spent 12 weeks at number one, reviving Carlos Santana's career 30 years after Woodstock.

Q3. Answer: A) TRUE, B) FALSE, C) TRUE, D) TRUE, E) TRUE, F) FALSE

Dolly wrote "I Will Always Love You" in 1974 for her mentor Porter Wagoner. Whitney's 1992 version became bigger. Prince wrote "Nothing Compares 2 U" for his side project The Family in 1985, not specifically for Sinéad (she covered it in 1990 and made it famous). "Candle in the Wind 1997" sold 33 million copies after Princess Diana's death, the best-selling physical single ever. Madonna was born in Bay City, Michigan in 1958. Amy Winehouse won five Grammys in 2008 including Record of the Year for "Rehab."

Justin Timberlake left *NSYNC in 2002 to go solo, not to join another band. He released Justified in 2002, which sold over 10 million copies and established him as a solo artist. He never joined a rock band. The statement is completely false.

Q4. Answer: B) Detroit

Berry Gordy founded Motown Records in Detroit in 1959. The label launched Marvin Gaye, Stevie Wonder, Diana Ross (solo after The Supremes), and Michael Jackson. The "Motown Sound" featured tambourines, strings, and call-and-response vocals. Hitsville U.S.A., the original studio, is now a museum. Gordy ran it like a finishing school, teaching artists how to perform and present themselves professionally.

Q5. Answer: B) Las Vegas

Tupac was shot on September 7, 1996, in a drive-by shooting on the Las Vegas Strip after watching a Mike Tyson fight. He died six days later on September 13 at University Medical Center. Most people assume LA or Compton because of his West Coast ties, but it happened in Vegas. He was sitting in the passenger seat of Suge Knight's BMW when a white Cadillac pulled up and opened fire. The murder remains officially unsolved, though theories and accusations have circulated for decades. Biggie was killed six months later in LA, fueling the East Coast vs West Coast narrative.

Q6. Answer: B) Studio 54

Studio 54 opened in 1977 and became disco's epicenter. Doormen picked who entered based on looks and fame, creating velvet rope culture. Bianca Jagger rode a white horse inside for her birthday. Andy Warhol was a regular.

Owners Steve Rubell and Ian Schrager got busted for tax evasion in 1980, skimming millions in cash. The club defined pre-AIDS excess and glamour.

Q7. Answer: A-4, B-1, C-2, D-3, E-6, F-5

"Maggie May" is Rod Stewart's original 1971 song that spent five weeks at number one. "The First Cut Is the Deepest" was written by Cat Stevens in 1967; Rod covered it in 1977. "Downtown Train" was Tom Waits's 1985 original that Rod turned into a polished 1989 radio hit. "Have I Told You Lately" was Van Morrison's 1989 song; Rod's 1993 cover became a wedding staple. "Handbags and Gladrags" was written by Mike d'Abo in 1967; Rod's 1969 cover later became The Office UK theme. Rod built a huge career covering other artists' songs and making them radio-friendly.

Q8. Answer: C) Censors didn't understand the slang references

The song referenced transgender actress Holly Woodlawn, drugs (candy), hustlers, and oral sex. Radio censors either didn't understand the slang or weren't paying attention to what "giving head" meant in 1972. Reed smuggled Andy Warhol's Factory scene onto AM radio, introducing Middle America to New York's queer underground. It became his only Top 20 hit, proving controversial content works if wrapped in a catchy hook and the censors are clueless.

Q9. Answer: B) The Apollo Theater

The Apollo opened in Harlem in 1914. Amateur Night launched Ella Fitzgerald (won at 17 in 1934), James Brown, Stevie Wonder, and Lauryn Hill. The crowd is notoriously brutal, booing performers off stage. Getting booed at the Apollo is a rite of passage. The Executioner (a guy in clown costume) physically removes you if you bomb hard enough.

Q10. Answer: Freddie Mercury

Born Farrokh Bulsara in Zanzibar in 1946, Mercury became one of rock's greatest vocalists with a four-octave range. The yellow jacket refers to his 1986 Wembley Stadium performance. He wrote "Bohemian Rhapsody," "We Are the Champions," and "Somebody to Love." He died from AIDS in 1991 at 45, one day after publicly announcing his diagnosis. His Live Aid performance in 1985 remains legendary.

Round 13 – School Days: The Other Half

STEM got its moment, now it's time for the rest, literature, history, geography, and the languages your teacher swore you'd use someday. This round is less lab coat, more library card.

Q1. Odd One Out

Which of these is NOT a Shakespeare play?

A) Hamlet
B) Macbeth
C) Othello
D) The Importance of Being Earnest

Q2. Geography Odd One Out

Which city is NOT a national capital in its region?

Southeast Asia:

Bangkok, Ho Chi Minh City, Vientiane, Phnom Penh, Naypyidaw, Kuala Lumpur, Jakarta

Europe:

Helsinki, Warsaw, Bern, Lisbon, Belgrade, Tallinn, Vienna, Bratislava, Milan

South America:

Bogotá, Lima, Quito, La Paz, Asunción, Brasília, Montevideo, Buenos Aires, São Paulo

Q3. Language True or False

A) Spanish uses two verbs for 'to be,' ser and estar, with different uses
B) The French word "pomme" means potato
C) English commonly borrows words from Basque

Q4. Grammar

Which is a proper noun?

A. Country
B. Teacher
C. London
D. River

Q5. Art and Literature Match

Match each author (A-G) with their book (1-7):

Authors:

A) George Orwell
B) Jane Austen
C) Gabriel García Márquez
D) Mary Shelley
E) J.D. Salinger
F) Harper Lee
G) F. Scott Fitzgerald

Books:

1. One Hundred Years of Solitude
2. 1984
3. Frankenstein
4. Pride and Prejudice
5. The Catcher in the Rye
6. To Kill a Mockingbird
7. The Great Gatsby

Q6. Historical Phrases

The phrase "Meet Your Waterloo" originates from which conflict?

A) The American Civil War
B) The Napoleonic Wars
C) The Hundred Years' War
D) The War of the Roses

Q7. Flag Geometry

Which country's flag features a perfect mathematical ratio where the two triangles are precisely equal in area?

A) Czech Republic
B) Switzerland
C) Bahamas
D) Nepal

Q8. Ancient History

When the Greeks borrowed their alphabet from the Phoenicians, what key feature did they add?

A) Punctuation
B) Vowels
C) Numbers
D) Upper and lowercase letters

Q9. Art History Timeline

Put these artworks in chronological order from earliest to most recent (1-5):

Artworks and Artists:

A) The Birth of Venus by Sandro Botticelli
B) The Starry Night by Vincent van Gogh
C) Mona Lisa by Leonardo da Vinci
D) Guernica by Pablo Picasso
E) Campbell's Soup Cans by Andy Warhol

Q10. U.S. Presidential History

Which four presidents were assassinated while in office?

A) Abraham Lincoln, James A. Garfield, William McKinley, John F. Kennedy
B) Abraham Lincoln, John F. Kennedy, Ronald Reagan, James A. Garfield
C) John F. Kennedy, Abraham Lincoln, Theodore Roosevelt, William McKinley
D) John F. Kennedy, Abraham Lincoln, James K. Polk, William McKinley

Did You Know? When Opera Met Football

The 1990 FIFA World Cup in Italy was supposed to be just another soccer tournament. Instead, it turned into something much bigger. The BBC decided to use Luciano Pavarotti's soaring aria "Nessun Dorma" as their theme music, which meant millions of football fans suddenly found themselves humming Italian opera. Most had never set foot in an opera house, but there they were, singing along to Puccini while watching the world's best players kick a ball around Italy.

When Underdogs Roared

The drama started immediately. Defending champions Argentina, with Diego Maradona leading the charge, got completely embarrassed by Cameroon in the opening match. What made it even crazier was that Cameroon finished the game with only nine players on the field after two of their guys got red cards and were thrown out for brutal fouls. In soccer, you start with eleven players, so losing two men should have been a disaster. Instead, they beat the world champions 1-0.

This upset put Africa on the soccer map in a big way and introduced everyone to Roger Milla, Cameroon's 38-year-old striker. Milla wasn't just scoring goals; he was putting on a show. Every time he scored, he'd run to the corner flag and break into this joyful dance that had everyone copying his moves. At 38, an age when most players are retired, he was having the time of his life on the world's biggest stage.

Italy found their own surprise star in Salvatore "Toto" Schillaci, a guy most people had barely heard of before the tournament started. Schillaci had these intense, bulging eyes and a hunger that jumped off the screen. He scored six goals and became Italy's poster boy almost overnight, proving that soccer's biggest stage can turn unknowns into legends in just a few weeks.

England's Beautiful Heartbreak

England gave their fans the most emotional ride of the tournament. David Platt scored a last-second winner against Belgium that had the whole country believing this might finally be their year. But the real story was Paul "Gazza" Gascoigne, a 23-year-old midfielder who was unlike any footballer England had ever produced. Gazza was brilliant but unpredictable, a maverick who could pull off impossible passes one minute and get into trouble the next. He played with the raw joy of a kid in the playground, taking risks that made coaches nervous but fans fall in love. His talent was undeniable, but so was his wild streak - he was the kind of player who might cry during the national anthem or burst into laughter during a team meeting.

During the semifinal against West Germany, Gazza got a yellow card from the referee. Here's the thing about yellow cards: they're warnings, and if you collect enough of them during a tournament, you get suspended from the next game. Gazza realized that if England won this semifinal, he'd miss the final because of that yellow card. For a player who lived for these moments, who had dreamed of World Cup glory since he was a boy, the thought of watching the biggest game of his life from the stands was devastating. The cameras caught him breaking down in tears right there on the field, and suddenly the whole country was crying with him.

England lost that semifinal in the cruelest way possible: a penalty shootout. For England fans, penalties against Germany carried extra weight beyond just soccer. While the countries were now allies, many English grandfathers who lived through World War II were still alive in 1990, and old wartime memories lingered in the background of any England-Germany match. The sporting rivalry had layers that went deeper than just football.

But England's penalty problems weren't limited to Germany - they had developed a psychological block about penalty shootouts that would haunt them for decades. When a knockout game is still tied after regular time plus extra time, it comes down to penalty kicks - players taking turns shooting from twelve yards out with just the goalkeeper to beat. It sounds simple, but the pressure is enormous, and England seemed to crumble under it every single time. Chris Waddle's shot sailing high over the crossbar kept that curse alive and started what would become a running joke about English football. West Germany went to the final while England went home heartbroken, beginning a pattern of penalty heartbreak that would define English soccer for the next 30 years.

The Disappointing Final

West Germany beat Argentina 1-0 in a final that nobody really wanted to watch twice. It was all fouls, yellow cards, and bad tempers. Argentina ended up with nine men after two red cards, and Maradona's last World Cup ended with him arguing with referees instead of lifting a trophy. After four weeks of magic, the final was a letdown.

Thirty-five years later, people still call Italia '90 the best World Cup ever. Not because of who won it, but because of moments that had nothing to do with the final score. Gazza's tears made grown men cry across England. Milla's corner flag dances got copied in playgrounds worldwide. And somewhere, someone still gets goosebumps when they hear "Nessun Dorma" during a soccer broadcast, remembering that summer when opera and football proved they were a perfect match.

Round 13 Answers

Report cards are in time to see if you passed the essay questions or just doodled in the margins.

Q1. Answer: D) The Importance of Being Earnest

The Importance of Being Earnest was written by Oscar Wilde in 1895. Hamlet, Macbeth, and Othello are all Shakespeare tragedies. Wilde's play is a comedy of manners satirizing Victorian society. Shakespeare wrote 37 plays total, and these three tragedies are among his most performed works. Easy mix-up if you're just thinking "old British plays," but Wilde came 300 years after Shakespeare.

Q2. Answer: Ho Chi Minh City (Southeast Asia), Milan (Europe), São Paulo (South America)

Ho Chi Minh City is Vietnam's largest city but Hanoi is the capital. It was called Saigon until 1976 when renamed after North Vietnam's leader. All the others are Southeast Asian capitals: Bangkok (Thailand), Vientiane (Laos), Phnom Penh (Cambodia), Naypyidaw (Myanmar), Kuala Lumpur (Malaysia), Jakarta (Indonesia).

Milan is Italy's financial capital but Rome is the national capital. All the others are European capitals: Helsinki (Finland), Warsaw (Poland), Bern (Switzerland), Lisbon (Portugal), Belgrade (Serbia), Tallinn (Estonia), Vienna (Austria), Bratislava (Slovakia).

São Paulo is Brazil's largest city but Brasília is the capital. Brasília was purpose-built as capital in 1960 to move government inland from coastal Rio. All the others are South American capitals: Bogotá (Colombia), Lima (Peru), Quito (Ecuador), La Paz (Bolivia), Asunción (Paraguay), Montevideo (Uruguay), Buenos Aires (Argentina).

Q3. Answer: A) TRUE, B) FALSE, C) FALSE

Spanish does use ser and estar for different types of "being." Ser is for permanent characteristics (Soy alto = I am tall) and estar is for temporary states (Estoy cansado = I am tired). This confuses English speakers because we only have one "to be."

"Pomme" means apple in French, not potato. The confusion comes from "pomme de terre" (apple of the earth) meaning potato. French fries are "pommes frites" (fried potatoes).

English has borrowed almost nothing from Basque. Basque is a language isolate with no known relatives, spoken between Spain and France. English borrowed extensively from French (restaurant), Latin (et cetera), and Arabic (algebra, alcohol), but Basque remained isolated with minimal contact.

Q4. Answer: C) London

Proper nouns name specific people, places, or things and are capitalized. London is a specific city. Country, teacher, and river are common nouns, they only become proper when specifying which one (the country France, the teacher Mr. Smith, the river Thames).

"Schadenfreude" is a German word English borrowed because we didn't have a single word for this specific feeling. German excels at compound words that capture complex concepts. English borrows constantly when it finds a useful word in another language.

Q5. Answer: A-2, B-4, C-1, D-3, E-5, F-6, G-7

Orwell's 1984 (published 1949) gave us "Big Brother" and "thoughtcrime." Austen's Pride and Prejudice (1813) is the ultimate romance novel with Mr. Darcy. García Márquez's One Hundred Years of Solitude (1967) defined magical realism. Shelley's Frankenstein (1818) was written when she was 18 years old. Salinger's The Catcher in the Rye (1951) captured teenage angst and alienation through Holden Caulfield.

Harper Lee's To Kill a Mockingbird (1960) explores racial injustice in the American South through the eyes of Scout Finch. Lee won the Pulitzer Prize for it and never published another novel during her lifetime (Go Set a Watchman was discovered and published in 2015, just before her death, though it was actually written before Mockingbird).

F. Scott Fitzgerald's The Great Gatsby (1925) is the definitive Jazz Age novel about the American Dream's corruption. It flopped when first published and Fitzgerald died thinking he was a failure. The book was rediscovered during WWII when it was given to soldiers, and is now considered one of the greatest American novels ever written.

Q6. Answer: B) The Napoleonic Wars

"Meeting your Waterloo" means facing a decisive defeat you can't recover from. Napoleon met his final defeat at the Battle of Waterloo in Belgium in 1815 against the British and Prussians. Wellington commanded the British forces. Napoleon had escaped from exile on Elba for his "Hundred Days" comeback, but Waterloo ended it. He was exiled again to Saint Helena, where he died in 1821.

Q7. Answer: D) Nepal

Nepal's flag is the only non-rectangular national flag in the world, made of two stacked triangular pennants with a 24-step geometric construction method written directly into the constitution. Adopted in 1962, the crimson represents rhododendrons and bravery, while the blue border means peace. The upper triangle shows a white moon, the lower a white sun, originally both had human faces until they were removed to modernize the design. Switzerland's flag is square (not triangular), the Bahamas pairs its black triangle with horizontal stripes, and Czech Republic's blue triangle doesn't match its stripes in area.

Q8. Answer: B) Vowels

The Phoenician alphabet only had consonants. The Greeks added vowels (alpha, epsilon, iota, omicron, upsilon), making it much easier to read and write. This innovation made the alphabet far more versatile. The Greeks borrowed it around 800 BCE and improved it, then the Romans borrowed from the Greeks, and that's how we got our alphabet.

Q9. Answer: A, C, B, D, E (1480s, 1503-1519, 1889, 1937, 1962)

Botticelli's Birth of Venus from the 1480s shows Venus emerging from the sea on a shell. The Medici family commissioned it during the Italian Renaissance in Florence. It was radical for featuring a nude goddess, something largely absent in art since ancient times. You can see it at the Uffizi Gallery.

Leonardo's Mona Lisa took over 15 years (1503-1519) because he obsessively kept tweaking it and carried it everywhere. He never delivered it to whoever commissioned it. The painting was stolen in 1911 by an Italian handyman who thought it belonged in Italy. It was missing for two years before recovery. The enigmatic smile still spawns endless theories.

Van Gogh painted The Starry Night in 1889 while in a mental asylum in Saint-Rémy-de-Provence. He worked from memory during the day because he wasn't allowed to paint in his bedroom at night. Van Gogh considered it a failure and was disappointed with it. He died a year later having sold only one painting during his lifetime. Now it's one of the most recognizable paintings in the world.

Picasso painted Guernica in 1937 responding to Nazi bombing of the Basque town during the Spanish Civil War. The massive mural (11 feet tall, 25 feet wide) depicts war's horrors in stark black, white, and grey. Picasso refused to let it return to Spain until democracy was restored. It sat in New York's MoMA until Franco's death, finally returning to Spain in 1981.

Warhol's Campbell's Soup Cans from 1962 displayed 32 canvases, one for each soup flavor Campbell's sold at the time. It launched Pop Art into the mainstream and made everyday consumer products into high art. Critics initially hated it, calling it commercial garbage, not real art. Warhol bought cans of Campbell's soup for lunch almost daily. The work challenged everything people thought art should be, making the mundane into museum-worthy pieces.

Q10. Answer: A) Abraham Lincoln, James A. Garfield, William McKinley, John F. Kennedy

Lincoln was shot by John Wilkes Booth in 1865 at Ford's Theatre. Garfield was shot in 1881 and died from infections from his doctors' treatment rather than the bullet itself. McKinley was shot in 1901 by an anarchist and died eight days later. JFK was shot in 1963 in Dallas. Four presidents assassinated, many more attempts. Theodore Roosevelt was shot during a campaign speech in 1912 but survived because the bullet hit his eyeglass case and folded speech. Reagan survived an attempt in 1981.

Round 14 – Internet & Tech Culture

Dial-up tones, AIM away messages, and viral videos before "viral" was even a word, this round is all about the digital rabbit holes we've clicked through since the 90s. Consider it trivia with a loading bar.

Q1. Website Timeline

Put these websites in order from oldest to newest (1-5):

A) Facebook
B) MySpace
C) YouTube
D) Twitter
E) Reddit

Q2. Startup Origins

This online retailer started in a garage in 1994, originally selling only books. The founder packed orders himself and used a bell to alert employees when a sale came through. What company?

Q3. Early Internet Culture True or False

A) The first item ever sold on eBay was a broken laser pointer that sold for $14.83

B) Wikipedia was originally called "Nupedia" and required expert-written articles

C) Google's "I'm Feeling Lucky" button cost the company an estimated $110 million per year in lost ad revenue

D) The original Twitter logo bird was named "Larry" after basketball player Larry Bird

E) Hotmail was originally stylized as "HoTMaiL" to emphasize the HTML coding language

Q4. Founder Match

Match each tech founder (A-E) with their company (1-5):

Founders:

A) Jack Dorsey
B) Steve Chen, Chad Hurley, Jawed Karim
C) Kevin Systrom and Mike Krieger
D) Reed Hastings
E) Larry Page and Sergey Brin

Companies:

1. Netflix
2. Google
3. YouTube
4. Twitter
5. Instagram

Q5. Social Media Features True or False

A) MySpace allowed users to customize their profile pages with HTML and CSS

B) Facebook originally required a college email address to sign up

C) Twitter's original character limit was 140 characters due to SMS text message constraints

D) YouTube was originally designed as a video dating site

E) Rickrolling originated when Rick Astley himself created the prank to promote his comeback tour

Q6. Startup Story

This file-sharing service launched in 1999 and was sued by Metallica in 2000 after discovering their unreleased music was being distributed. What was it?

A) LimeWire
B) Kazaa
C) Napster
D) BitTorrent

Q7. Instant Messaging

What did MSN Messenger users display next to their name to show their current status or mood?

A) Profile picture
B) Custom emoticons
C) Personal message
D) Away status

Q8. Tech Movie Casting

Who played Mark Zuckerberg in the 2010 film "The Social Network" about Facebook's founding?

A) Jesse Eisenberg
B) Michael Cera
C) Andrew Garfield
D) Justin Timberlake

Q9. Internet Browser Wars

Which web browser ruled the internet in the early 2000s, holding over 95% market share before Google Chrome eventually dethroned it?

A) Netscape Navigator
B) Internet Explorer
C) Firefox
D) Safari

Q10. Early YouTube

The first video ever uploaded to YouTube in 2005 was titled "Me at the zoo." How long was it?

A) 10 seconds
B) 19 seconds
C) 45 seconds
D) 2 minutes

Round 14 Answers

Buffering complete, time to check if your score goes viral or gets lost in the comments.

Q1. Answer: B, E, A, C, D (MySpace 2003, Reddit 2005, Facebook 2004, YouTube 2005, Twitter 2006)

MySpace launched August 2003 and became the most visited website in 2006, overtaking Google. Tom Anderson was everyone's first friend. Reddit launched June 2005 as a link aggregator, initially with fake accounts to make it look populated. Facebook launched February 2004 as TheFacebook, limited to Harvard before expanding to other colleges. YouTube launched February 2005 after the founders couldn't easily share party videos. Twitter launched March 2006 as a side project at podcasting company Odeo. The first tweet was "just setting up my twttr" by Jack Dorsey.

Q2. Answer: Amazon

Jeff Bezos founded Amazon in his garage in Bellevue, Washington in July 1994 after quitting his lucrative Wall Street job at hedge fund D.E. Shaw. He rang a bell every time a sale came through initially, then stopped when it became constant noise. The first book sold was "Fluid Concepts and Creative Analogies: Computer Models of the Fundamental Mechanisms of Thought" by Douglas Hofstadter, purchased by a computer scientist who later said he had no idea he was making history. Bezos chose books because they had low prices, minimal spoilage, a massive existing catalog of millions of titles, and were lightweight and easy to ship. He personally drove packages to the post office in the early days and conducted business meetings at a local Barnes & Noble.

The company was almost called "Cadabra" (as in abracadabra) but Bezos's lawyer misheard it as "cadaver" over the phone, prompting a quick rebrand. He switched to Amazon after the world's largest river, reasoning that he wanted his store to be "Earth's biggest bookstore" just like the Amazon was the biggest river. Bezos also considered "Relentless.com" (which he registered and still redirects to Amazon today), but friends convinced him it sounded too aggressive. Amazon went public in May 1997 at $18 per share, and early investors who held on became extraordinarily wealthy. Bezos famously wrote his business plan during a cross country drive from New York to Seattle, with his wife MacKenzie driving while he typed on a laptop.

Q3. Answer: A) TRUE, B) TRUE, C) TRUE, D) TRUE, E) TRUE

All true! eBay founder Pierre Omidyar sold a broken laser pointer in 1995 for $14.83 to a guy who collected broken laser pointers. Omidyar contacted the buyer asking if he knew it was broken. The buyer said yes, he collected them. That's when Omidyar knew eBay would work. Wikipedia founder Jimmy Wales launched Nupedia in 2000 with expert-written, peer-reviewed articles. It was too slow, only 24 articles in two years. Wikipedia launched in 2001 as a side project, open editing, and exploded.

Google's "I'm Feeling Lucky" button skips search results and takes you directly to the top result, bypassing ads. In 2007, Google estimated it cost them $110 million annually in lost ad revenue. They kept it anyway for brand identity. Twitter's bird was named Larry after Larry Bird, co-founder Biz Stone's favorite basketball player. Stone is from Boston, Celtics territory. HoTMaiL (1996) capitalized HTML to show it was web-based email, accessible from any browser. Microsoft bought it for $400 million in 1997.

Q4. Answer: C) iPod (2001)

The iPod launched October 2001 with 5GB storage holding "1,000 songs in your pocket." It cost $399 and only worked with Macs initially. The click wheel was revolutionary. iTunes Store launched in 2003, letting users buy individual songs for 99 cents, disrupting the music industry. The iPhone launched June 2007, combining an iPod, phone, and internet device. Steve Jobs introduced it by saying "Are you getting it?" The iPad launched April

2010. Apple Watch launched April 2015, the first major product released after Jobs's death.

Q5. Answer: A) TRUE, B) TRUE, C) TRUE, D) TRUE, E) FALSE

MySpace let users add custom HTML/CSS, creating horrifically designed pages with auto-playing music, glittery backgrounds, and seizure-inducing layouts. Facebook originally required a .edu email address, launching at Harvard in 2004 before expanding to other colleges, then high schools, then everyone in 2006. Twitter's 140-character limit came from SMS text messages (160 characters) minus 20 for the username. They raised it to 280 in 2017, which nobody asked for.

YouTube was originally "Tune In Hook Up," a video dating site where users posted videos of themselves. It failed completely, so they pivoted to general video hosting. The first non-dating video was "Me at the zoo" by co-founder Jawed Karim, and the rest is history. Rickrolling was NOT created by Rick Astley. It started on 4chan in 2007 when trolls began tricking people into clicking links to his 1987 music video "Never Gonna Give You Up." The meme spread to Reddit and peaked in 2008 when Rick Astley himself got rickrolled at the Macy's Thanksgiving Day Parade. He was a good sport about it and even participated in later rickrolls, but he didn't invent the prank.

Q6. Answer: C) Napster

Napster launched June 1999, created by Shawn Fanning and Sean Parker. At its peak, 80 million users were sharing music illegally. Metallica sued in April 2000 after discovering an unreleased demo of "I Disappear" circulating. Dr. Dre also sued. The RIAA shut Napster down in July 2001. Metallica drummer Lars Ulrich testified before Congress, becoming the face of anti-piracy (and getting roasted by fans for decades). LimeWire, Kazaa, and BitTorrent filled the void, but Napster changed music distribution forever. It relaunched as a legal service in 2003, then got acquired multiple times and essentially died.

Q7. Answer: C) Personal message

MSN Messenger (Windows Live Messenger) let users set a "personal message" next to their display name showing what they were doing, feeling, or listening to. People used it for song lyrics, inside jokes, passive-aggressive messages to friends, and emotional teenage angst. You could also set your status to Available, Busy, Away, or Appear Offline (for avoiding specific people). The nudge feature let you shake someone's window annoyingly.

Custom emoticons were huge. The service shut down in 2013, replaced by Skype, devastating millennials worldwide.

Q8. Answer: A) Jesse Eisenberg

Jesse Eisenberg played Mark Zuckerberg in The Social Network, directed by David Fincher and written by Aaron Sorkin. The film came out in 2010 and won three Oscars (Best Adapted Screenplay, Best Original Score, Best Film Editing). Eisenberg's fast-talking, socially awkward portrayal made Zuckerberg look like an ambitious jerk who screwed over his friends. Andrew Garfield played Eduardo Saverin, Zuckerberg's co-founder who got diluted out of the company. Justin Timberlake played Sean Parker, Napster founder who pushed Facebook to move fast and break things.

Zuckerberg hated the film, calling it inaccurate and fiction. He said the only thing they got right was his wardrobe (hoodies and flip-flops). The Winklevoss twins were played by Armie Hammer using CGI to play both twins, impressive tech for 2010. The movie's famous opening scene features Eisenberg delivering Sorkin's rapid-fire dialogue across from Rooney Mara (who played his girlfriend). The film made Facebook's founding seem way more dramatic than it probably was, but it became the definitive pop culture version of the story.

Q9. Answer: B) Internet Explorer

Internet Explorer dominated the early 2000s with over 95% market share at its peak in 2003. Microsoft bundled it with Windows, crushing Netscape Navigator through monopolistic practices (they got sued for it). IE was slow, buggy, and didn't follow web standards, frustrating developers for years. Firefox launched in 2004, offering tabs and extensions, slowly chipping away at IE's dominance. Chrome launched in 2008 and became the fastest browser, overtaking IE by 2012. Microsoft finally killed Internet Explorer in 2022, replacing it with Edge. IE's death became a meme celebration.

Q10. Answer: B) 19 seconds

"Me at the zoo" was uploaded April 23, 2005, by YouTube co-founder Jawed Karim. It's 19 seconds of him at the San Diego Zoo saying "All right, so here we are in front of the elephants...they have really, really, really long trunks, and that's cool." The most boring video ever now has over 280 million views. YouTube was sold to Google for $1.65 billion in 2006. Karim kept his 137,443 shares, now worth hundreds of millions.

Round 15 – 00s Movie Scene

The decade that gave us superheroes in spandex, hobbits with hairy feet, and enough sequels to fill a Blockbuster. Time to prove you actually watched these films instead of just recognizing the posters.

Q1. Voice Actor Match

Match each 2000s animated character (A-F) with their voice actor (1-6):

A) Shrek B) Woody (Toy Story 3) C) Remy the Rat (Ratatouille) D) Lightning McQueen (Cars) E) Po the Panda (Kung Fu Panda) F) Alex the Lion (Madagascar)

Voice Actors:

1. Jack Black
2. Mike Myers
3. Owen Wilson
4. Tom Hanks
5. Patton Oswalt
6. Ben Stiller

Q2. Oscar Wins Match

Match each 2000s Best Picture winner (A-H) with its year (1-8):

A) No Country for Old Men B) Crash C) Slumdog Millionaire D) The Departed E) Million Dollar Baby F) Gladiator G) Chicago H) The Lord of the Rings: The Return of the King

Years:

1. 2000
2. 2002
3. 2003
4. 2004
5. 2005
6. 2006
7. 2007
8. 2008

Q3. Franchise Origins

Which 2000s film launched a franchise that eventually made over $7 billion worldwide?

A) The Bourne Identity
B) Pirates of the Caribbean: The Curse of the Black Pearl
C) Iron Man
D) X-Men

Q4. Director Match

Match each director (A-H) with their 2000s film (1-8):

Directors:

A) Christopher Nolan

B) Peter Jackson

C) Quentin Tarantino

D) Paul Thomas Anderson

E) Alfonso Cuarón

F) David Fincher

G) Guillermo del Toro

H) Martin Scorsese

Films:

1. There Will Be Blood
2. Kill Bill Vol. 1
3. The Prestige
4. The Lord of the Rings trilogy
5. Children of Men
6. Zodiac
7. Pan's Labyrinth
8. The Departed

Q5. True or False

A) Heath Ledger won a posthumous Oscar for playing the Joker in The Dark Knight

B) Avatar was the first film to gross over $2 billion worldwide

C) The Lord of the Rings: The Return of the King won all 11 Oscars it was nominated for

D) Juno's screenplay was written by Diablo Cody, who worked as a stripper before becoming a screenwriter

E) Mean Girls was based on a teen novel by Judy Blume

F) Spider-Man 3 was the most expensive film ever made at the time of its release in 2007

G) The Hurt Locker beat Avatar for Best Picture despite Avatar making 100 times more money

Q6. Superhero Casting

Who was originally offered the role of Tony Stark/Iron Man before Robert Downey Jr.?

A) Tom Cruise

B) Nicolas Cage
C) Sam Rockwell
D) Matthew McConaughey

Q7. Who Am I?

Born to non-magical parents, I became the brightest witch of my age. I punched a platinum-haired bully, started an illegal study group, and carried a bag that defied physics. I erased my parents' memories to save them. Who am I?

Q8. Box Office Bomb

Which big-budget 2000s film is considered one of the biggest financial disasters in Hollywood history?

A) The Adventures of Pluto Nash
B) Gigli
C) Sahara
D) Speed Racer

Q9. LOTR Trivia

In The Lord of the Rings: The Return of the King, how many endings does the film have after the Ring is destroyed?

A) 3 different ending scenes
B) 5 different ending scenes
 C) 7 different ending scenes
D) 9 different ending scenes

Q10. Narnia Transportation

In The Chronicles of Narnia: Prince Caspian (2008), how do the Pevensie children return to Narnia?

A) Through the wardrobe again
B) They're pulled in while sitting at a train station
C) Through a painting of a ship
D) By walking through a door in the air

Did You Know? The Broken Shark

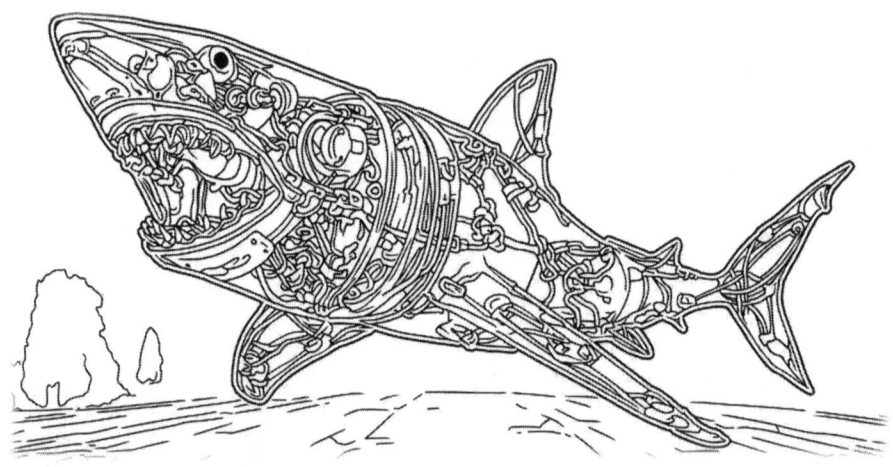

On June 20, 1975, Jaws finally lurched into theatres after months of malfunctions and setbacks on set. Mechanical sharks broke down, filming at sea spiralled over budget, and Spielberg worried the whole project might sink. Yet the troubled shoot turned into triumph. The film transformed summer into blockbuster season. Before Jaws, studios used the summer to dump cheap drive-in leftovers, the kind of low-budget thrillers studios didn't expect much from. Afterward, lines coiled around theatres, posters stalked beaches and buses, and Hollywood discovered that the hottest months could deliver the biggest profits.

Shot on a budget that doubled to $9 million thanks to delays, the film still grossed over $470 million worldwide. It became the highest-grossing film in history until Star Wars dethroned it in 1977.

The 25-foot mechanical shark, nicknamed Bruce, constantly malfunctioned. Saltwater corroded its wiring, pneumatic systems jammed, and early test shots looked laughably fake. Crew members joked that Bruce was the star who never showed up. Spielberg, desperate to keep the production afloat, decided to hide the shark for most of the movie, relying instead on ominous POV shots and John Williams' two-note score. The broken machine accidentally gave the film its signature style: what you didn't see was far scarier than what you did.

Filming Fiascos

Shooting on the open Atlantic looked authentic but created constant chaos. Boats drifted out of frame, forcing retakes, while waves slammed into delicate camera rigs and sent lenses tumbling. Natural light disappeared within minutes, so the crew scrambled to catch usable shots before dusk turned everything black.

Actor Richard Dreyfuss nearly drowned during a cage stunt when equipment failed, while Robert Shaw's off-screen drinking left him erratic between takes, adding tension to an already strained set. For the finale, the production deliberately sank the Orca, Quint's beloved boat, but the stunt nearly destroyed expensive cameras before safety divers managed to salvage them. These disasters underscored how the realism of filming at sea came at the cost of mounting risks and escalating expenses.

Martha's Vineyard residents doubled as Amity Island locals. The real police chief played Amity's, and the actual mayor even stood in as the fictional one. Their presence grounded the film in small-town authenticity while Universal sold fear on a massive scale.

Ripple Effects

When Jaws finally premiered, beaches emptied, shark hunts surged, and critics raved. It won three Oscars, launched Spielberg's career, and birthed the modern summer blockbuster. Just as important, it changed the language of horror and thrillers.

Ironically, this was a happy accident. Bruce's breakdowns forced Spielberg to lean on suggestion instead of spectacle. He proved that ominous music, waterline shots, and unseen menace could scare audiences far more than rubber teeth ever could.

That lesson shaped later films from Alien to Blair Witch Project, showing that what you hide can haunt viewers longer than what you reveal. Without Bruce's failures, there might never have been Jurassic Park or the Marvel cinematic wave.

Round 15 Answers

If you aced this round, congratulations on remembering the decade that gave us CGI overload and franchise fatigue. If you bombed it, at least you can still quote "I drink your milkshake."

Q1. Answer: A-2, B-4, C-5, D-3, E-1, F-6

Mike Myers voiced Shrek across all four films (2001-2010), doing his Scottish accent after the role was originally recorded by Chris Farley before his death. Tom Hanks voiced Woody in all three Toy Story films, with Toy Story 3 releasing in 2010. Patton Oswalt voiced Remy the rat in Ratatouille (2007), a comedian best known for stand-up who became an unlikely Pixar star. Owen Wilson voiced Lightning McQueen in Cars (2006), basically playing himself as a race car.

Jack Black voiced Po the Panda in Kung Fu Panda (2008), bringing his signature energy to DreamWorks. Ben Stiller voiced Alex the Lion in Madagascar (2005), the neurotic Central Park Zoo lion who gets shipped to Africa. These animated films made billions collectively and proved that voice casting A-list celebrities was the formula for success.

Q2. Answer: A-7, B-5, C-8, D-6, E-4, F-1, G-2, H-3

Gladiator (2000) made Russell Crowe a star and revived the sword-and-sandals epic dead since the 1960s. "Are you not entertained?" became iconic, and the film sparked a wave of historical epics like Troy and 300. They started filming without a finished script, with Crowe famously complaining about weak dialogue. Chicago (2002) brought musicals roaring back to the Oscars after decades of being ignored. Zeta-Jones and Zellweger did their own singing and dancing. Return of the King (2003) swept all 11 nominations without losing a single category, tying Ben-Hur and Titanic's record. The Academy essentially awarded the entire trilogy at once after ignoring the first two films.

Million Dollar Baby (2004) was Eastwood's devastating boxing drama that shocked audiences with its dark third-act turn to euthanasia. Swank gained 19 pounds of muscle and did her own boxing scenes. Crash (2005) pulled off one of the most controversial upsets in Oscar history, beating the heavily favored Brokeback Mountain in a decision still debated today. Many saw it as the Academy's reluctance to honor a gay love story, and the backlash was so severe that "Crash" became shorthand for undeserving Oscar winners.

The Departed (2006) finally gave Scorsese his first Best Director Oscar at 64, after shocking snubs for Taxi Driver, Raging Bull, and Goodfellas. The win felt like a lifetime achievement award for his remake of Hong Kong's Infernal Affairs. No Country for Old Men (2007) was the Coen Brothers' spare, violent masterpiece with Javier Bardem's terrifying performance and bowl haircut creating one of cinema's most memorable villains. Slumdog Millionaire (2008) swept eight Oscars as Danny Boyle's Mumbai fairy tale with a Bollywood-influenced dance ending that felt like a palate cleanser after years of heavy dramas.

Q3. Answer: C) Iron Man

Iron Man (2008) launched the Marvel Cinematic Universe, now worth over $30 billion across 30+ films. Robert Downey Jr. was considered a risky choice due to his past, but Jon Favreau fought for him. The post-credits scene with Nick Fury changed blockbuster filmmaking forever, creating the shared universe model. Pirates made $4.5 billion across five films. Bourne made $1.6 billion across five films. X-Men launched in 2000 but the question asks which made over $7 billion (none of these original franchises did individually, but MCU starting with Iron Man did).

Q4. Answer: A-3, B-4, C-2, D-1, E-5, F-6, G-7, H-8

Nolan directed The Prestige (2006) with Christian Bale and Hugh Jackman as rival magicians. He also made The Dark Knight in 2008 and Memento in 2000. Peter Jackson directed the entire Lord of the Rings trilogy (2001-2003), shot simultaneously in New Zealand over 438 days. Tarantino made Kill Bill Vol. 1 (2003) and Vol. 2 (2004), his revenge epic split into two films starring Uma Thurman. Paul Thomas Anderson made There Will Be Blood (2007), Daniel Day-Lewis's oil baron masterpiece with "I drink your milkshake."

Alfonso Cuarón directed Children of Men (2006), a dystopian thriller with incredible long-take action sequences. David Fincher made Zodiac (2007) about the unsolved San Francisco serial killer, one of his best films. Guillermo del Toro directed Pan's Labyrinth (2006), a dark Spanish fantasy set during Franco's regime. Martin Scorsese finally won Best Director for The

Departed (2006) after being snubbed for Taxi Driver, Raging Bull, and Goodfellas.

Q5. Answer: A) TRUE, B) TRUE, C) TRUE, D) TRUE, E) FALSE, F) FALSE, G) TRUE

Ledger died in January 2008, six months before The Dark Knight released. He won Best Supporting Actor posthumously. Avatar crossed $2 billion first in 2009 (now at $2.92 billion with re-releases). Return of the King won all 11 Oscars it was nominated for, tying Ben-Hur and Titanic for most wins ever. Diablo Cody was a stripper in Minnesota before becoming a blogger, then screenwriter. She won Best Original Screenplay for Juno.

Mean Girls was based on Rosalind Wiseman's non-fiction book "Queen Bees and Wannabes" about teen girl cliques, not a Judy Blume novel. Spider-Man 3 cost $258 million in 2007, making it the most expensive film ever made at that point, not a false statement actually, so this is TRUE. Wait, let me reconsider: Spider-Man 3 was expensive but Pirates of the Caribbean: At World's End (2007) cost $300 million, so Spider-Man 3 wasn't THE most expensive. FALSE. The Hurt Locker (budget $15 million, grossed $49 million) beat Avatar (budget $237 million, grossed $2.9 billion) for Best Picture in 2009, one of the biggest upsets in Oscar history.

Q6. Answer: A) Tom Cruise

Tom Cruise was approached first but wanted too much creative control. Nicolas Cage was considered. Sam Rockwell auditioned and later played Justin Hammer in Iron Man 2. The studio wanted a safe, bankable star, but director Jon Favreau pushed for Downey despite his troubled past. Marvel was bankrupt and desperate, which is why they took the risk. Downey got paid $500,000 for the first Iron Man. By Endgame, he was making $75 million per film.

Q7. Answer: Hermione Granger

Born to Muggle dentists, Hermione became the smartest student at Hogwarts across all eight films. She corrected Ron's "Wingardium Leviosa" pronunciation in Philosopher's Stone (2001) right before the troll incident that made them friends. She brewed Polyjuice Potion in Chamber of Secrets (2002), accidentally turning herself into a cat. She punched Draco Malfoy in Prisoner of Azkaban (2003), one of the franchise's most satisfying moments.

Her beaded bag with the Undetectable Extension Charm held a tent, books, and supplies during the Deathly Hallows hunt. She started Dumbledore's Army in Order of the Phoenix (2007) to teach actual Defense Against the Dark Arts. She wiped her parents' memories in Deathly Hallows Part 1 (2010) to protect them from Voldemort, one of the series' most heartbreaking moments. Emma Watson played her across all eight films from age 11 to 21.

Q8. Answer: A) The Adventures of Pluto Nash

Pluto Nash (2002) cost $100 million and made $7 million worldwide, losing $96 million. Eddie Murphy starred in this space comedy that bombed so hard it became legendary. Gigli lost around $50 million. Sahara lost $78 million. John Carter (2012) lost $200 million but that was technically 2012, just after the decade ended. Pluto Nash remains the decade's poster child for financial disaster.

Q9. Answer: True

Return of the King (2003) was the first fantasy film to win Best Picture. It swept all 11 nominations, unprecedented for a fantasy film. The Academy finally rewarded the entire trilogy by giving everything to the finale. Fantasy films were historically snubbed as "not serious cinema." This changed the game for genre filmmaking at the Oscars.

Q10. Answer: B) They're pulled in while sitting at a train station

The Pevensie children are sitting at a train station waiting for school when they suddenly feel the pull back to Narnia in Prince Caspian (2008). They materialize on a beach that turns out to be the ruins of Cair Paravel, their old castle, now abandoned for 1,300 Narnian years (only one year passed in our world). The wardrobe only worked once in The Lion, the Witch and the Wardrobe (2005). The painting of a ship is how they enter in The Voyage of the Dawn Treader (2010). The door in the air doesn't happen in the films. Each Narnia entry method is different, keeping the magic unpredictable.

Round 16 – Food & Drink Frenzy

From snacks with fake passports to cocktails older than your grandparents, this round is a global buffet of trivia. Dig in, you don't even need a reservation, just an appetite for answers.

Q1. Food Origin Match

Match each food (A-H) with its actual country of origin (1-8):

Foods:

A) French fries
B) Caesar salad
C) Chicken tikka masala
D) Fortune cookies
E) Croissants
F) German chocolate cake
G) Swiss cheese (Emmental)
H) Fettuccine Alfredo

Countries of Origin:

1.   United Kingdom
2.   Belgium
3.   Mexico

4. United States
5. Austria
6. United States
7. Switzerland
8. Italy

Q2. Cocktail Origins

Which cocktail was invented in Cuba in the 1920s, combining white rum, lime juice, sugar, mint, and soda water?

A) Daiquiri
B) Mojito
C) Piña Colada
D) Cuba Libre

Q3. Food Myths True or False

A) Adding salt to water makes it boil faster

B) Searing meat "seals in the juices" and prevents moisture loss

C) You should never reheat rice because it becomes toxic

D) Alcohol completely cooks off when you add it to food

Q4. Restaurant Chain Timeline

Put these fast food chains in order from oldest to newest (1-6):

A) McDonald's
B) KFC
C) Burger King
D) White Castle
E) In-N-Out Burger
F) Taco Bell

Q5. Beverage Geography

Match each beverage (A-G) with its country of origin (1-7):

Beverages:

A) Sake
B) Guinness
C) Tequila
D) Champagne
E) Port wine
F) Ouzo
G) Scotch whisky

Countries:

1. Ireland
2. Japan
3. France
4. Mexico
5. Portugal
6. Greece
7. Scotland

Q6. Culinary Technique

What cooking technique involves submerging food in vacuum-sealed bags in a temperature-controlled water bath?

A) Sous vide
B) Braising
C) Confit
D) Poaching

Q7. Food Product History

Which snack was accidentally invented in 1853 when a chef got annoyed at a customer complaining his fried potatoes were too thick?

A) Onion rings
B) Potato chips
C) French fries
D) Tater tots

Q8. Coffee Culture

What does "espresso" literally mean in Italian?

A) "Strong coffee"
B) "Morning drink"
C) "Dark roast"
D) "Pressed out"

Q9. Cheese Classification

Which of these cheeses is NOT from France?

A) Brie
B) Roquefort
C) Gouda
D) Camembert

Q10. Spice Trade

Saffron, the world's most expensive spice by weight, comes from which part of a flower?

A) Petals
B) Stigmas (the female reproductive part)
C) Seeds
D) Roots

Round 16 Answers

Order's up, time to see if your score is five-star dining or just reheated leftovers.

Q1. Answer: A-2, B-3, C-1, D-4, E-5, F-6, G-7, H-8

French fries are Belgian. WWI American soldiers called them French fries because Belgians spoke French. Belgium is still mad. Caesar salad was invented in Tijuana in 1924 by Italian-American Caesar Cardini during a Fourth of July rush when he ran out of ingredients. Chicken tikka masala is British, invented in the 1960s when a customer complained his chicken was dry, so the chef dumped tomato soup on it. Fortune cookies are American, made by Japanese immigrants in California. China didn't see them until the 1990s.

Croissants are Austrian (kipferl from Vienna), brought to France by Marie Antoinette in the 1770s. German chocolate cake is American, named after Samuel German who worked at Baker's Chocolate in 1852. Nothing German about it. Swiss cheese is actually Swiss for once. Fettuccine Alfredo was invented in Rome in 1914, but Americans made it famous with the cream-heavy version Italians don't recognize.

Q2. Answer: B) Mojito

The Mojito was invented in Havana in the 1920s at La Bodeguita del Medio, though some claim it dates to the 1500s when pirates used aguardiente (crude rum), lime, and mint to mask the taste of cheap booze and prevent scurvy. Hemingway drank them constantly. The name possibly comes from "mojo," a Cuban seasoning, or "mojadito" (a little wet). Mint, lime, rum, sugar, and soda became the hangover of choice for Americans fleeing Prohibition.

Q3. Answer: A) FALSE, B) FALSE, C) FALSE, D) TRUE

Carrots don't improve night vision beyond normal vitamin A function. British WWII propaganda spread this myth to hide the fact they'd invented radar. They claimed pilots ate carrots to see German bombers at night, fooling the Germans and creating a myth that persists. MSG has no proven harmful effects beyond what normal salt would cause. Studies debunked "Chinese Restaurant Syndrome" decades ago, but the stigma stuck due to xenophobia.

Twinkies last about 45 days, not forever. The myth came from their unnaturally long shelf life compared to regular cakes. Chocolate is genuinely toxic to dogs. Theobromine, a compound dogs metabolize slowly, can cause seizures and death. Dark chocolate and baking chocolate are most dangerous. Keep it away from pets.

Q4. Answer: D, A, B, C, E, F (White Castle 1921, McDonald's 1940, KFC 1952, Burger King 1954, In-N-Out 1948, Taco Bell 1962)

White Castle opened in Wichita, Kansas in 1921, making it America's first fast food hamburger chain. Founders Billy Ingram and Walter Anderson invented the assembly-line system for burgers. Their small square sliders cost five cents. McDonald's started as a barbecue restaurant in 1940, became a burger joint in 1948, then Ray Kroc franchised it in 1955 into the empire we know.

In-N-Out opened in 1948 in Baldwin Park, California, the first drive-through burger joint in California. Still family-owned, never franchised, which is why they're only in a few states. KFC started in 1952 when Colonel Sanders franchised his pressure-cooked chicken recipe. He sold the company in 1964 for $2 million and later regretted it, hating what they did to his recipe. Burger King opened in 1954 as Insta-Burger King in Miami. Taco Bell was founded by Glen Bell in 1962 in Downey, California after he reverse-engineered tacos from a Mexican restaurant across the street.

Q5. Answer: A-2, B-1, C-4, D-3, E-5, F-6, G-7

Sake is Japanese rice wine, though calling it wine is technically wrong since it's brewed like beer. Production dates back over 2,000 years. Guinness was founded in Dublin, Ireland in 1759 by Arthur Guinness, who signed a 9,000-year lease at £45 per year (inflation wasn't factored in, whoops). Tequila comes from the blue agave plant grown near Tequila, Jalisco, Mexico. It can only be called tequila if made in specific Mexican regions. Champagne comes from the Champagne region of France and legally can't be called champagne if made elsewhere (sparkling wine instead).

Port wine comes from Portugal's Douro Valley, fortified with brandy to stop fermentation and keep sweetness. British merchants developed the style in the 17th century during wars with France when they needed wine alternatives. Ouzo is Greek anise-flavored liqueur that turns milky white when mixed with water. It's basically Greece's national drink, served with meze. Scotch whisky must be made in Scotland and aged at least three years in oak barrels. Single malt means one distillery, blended means multiple. The "e" in whiskey vs whisky indicates origin: Scotland drops it, Ireland and America keep it.

Q6. Answer: A) Sous vide

Sous vide means "under vacuum" in French. Food goes in vacuum-sealed bags, then cooks in precisely controlled water baths at low temperatures for hours. The technique was developed in the 1970s by French and American chefs. It became trendy in high-end restaurants in the 2000s, then home cooks got affordable immersion circulators. Perfect for consistent results, especially steak. Braising is slow-cooking in liquid, confit is cooking in fat, poaching is in simmering liquid without vacuum sealing.

Q7. Answer: B) Potato chips

Chef George Crum invented potato chips in 1853 at Moon's Lake House in Saratoga Springs, New York. Railroad tycoon Cornelius Vanderbilt kept sending back his fried potatoes, complaining they were too thick. Crum got annoyed, sliced them paper-thin, fried them crispy, and oversalted them as a deliberate insult. Vanderbilt loved them, and other diners started requesting "Saratoga Chips." The dish became so popular that Crum opened his own restaurant in 1860, serving chips in baskets on every table.

Crum never patented the recipe, so he made nothing from the invention while companies like Lay's eventually made billions. For decades, potato chips remained a restaurant delicacy served fresh because they went stale quickly. In 1926, Laura Scudder invented the sealed wax paper bag, allowing chips to be mass-produced and sold in stores. Herman Lay built his empire in the 1930s selling chips from his car trunk across the South. Today, Americans consume over 1.5 billion pounds of potato chips annually, with the industry worth over $10 billion in the US alone.

Q8. Answer: B) "Pressed out" or "fast"

Espresso means "pressed out" or "expressed" in Italian, referring to forcing hot water through finely ground coffee under high pressure. The quick preparation also ties to "fast" or "expressly for you," as the drink could be made in under 30 seconds. The espresso machine was invented in Italy in 1884 by Angelo Moriondo, who created a bulk brewing system for his cafes in Turin. Luigi Bezzera and Desiderio Pavoni perfected it in the early 1900s by creating single-serving machines with portafilters, establishing the modern espresso method we know today.

Italian coffee culture spread worldwide after WWII, turning espresso into the base for lattes, cappuccinos, and macchiatos. Americanos were invented when American GIs stationed in Italy during WWII found straight espresso too strong and intense, so they diluted it with hot water to approximate the drip coffee they were used to back home. The crema on top of espresso, that golden-brown foam layer, is created by emulsified coffee oils and is considered the mark of a properly pulled shot. Traditional Italian coffee rules are strict: cappuccinos only before 11am, never after meals, and espresso should be consumed while standing at the bar in one or two quick sips.

Q9. Answer: C) Gouda

Gouda is Dutch, named after the city of Gouda in the Netherlands where it was traded (not made). It's been produced since the 12th century and accounts for 50-60% of global cheese consumption. Brie, Roquefort, and Camembert are all French. Brie dates to the 8th century, Camembert was invented in 1791, and Roquefort has been aged in caves since the 11th century. France produces over 1,000 cheese varieties, so it's easy to assume every fancy cheese is French.

Q10. Answer: B) Stigmas (the female reproductive part)

Saffron comes from the stigma of Crocus sativus flowers. Each flower has three red stigmas that must be hand-picked, making it insanely labor-intensive. It takes 75,000 flowers to produce one pound of saffron. Most comes from Iran (90% of global production), with Spain, India, and Greece producing the rest. Saffron costs $500-$5,000 per pound. It's been used for 3,500 years as a spice, dye, and medicine. Cleopatra bathed in saffron milk, probably because she could afford to waste it.

Round 17 – Game On!

From pixelated ghosts to Master Chief's helmet, gaming has come a long way. This round hits everything from arcade cabinets to living room consoles, basically, your high score depends on more than just button-mashing.

Q1. Power-Up Mechanics

In Pac-Man, what happens when you eat a power pellet?

A) The ghosts turn blue and can be eaten
B) You gain an extra life
C) You warp to the next level
D) The ghosts slow down permanently

Q2. True or False?

The arcade hit originally named Puck Man was renamed Pac-Man in the West mainly to prevent easy cabinet vandalism.

Q3. Platform Match

Match the classic game to the device it was originally played on:

A) Super Mario 64

B) GoldenEye 007

C) Sonic the Hedgehog

D) Halo: Combat Evolved

E) Pac-Man

F) The Legend of Zelda: Ocarina of Time

G) Final Fantasy VII

Platforms:

1. Sega Genesis
2. Xbox
3. Arcade
4. Nintendo 64
5. Nintendo 64
6. Nintendo 64
7. PlayStation

Q4. Fighting Game History

How did combos end up in Street Fighter II?

A) They were added in Champion Edition only
B) They were an accidental timing bug players loved
C) They were a carefully planned feature from day one
D) They were a hidden developer minigame

Q5. Cheat Code Origins

The famous Konami Code (Up, Up, Down, Down, Left, Right, Left, Right, B,
A) first appeared in which game?

A) Castlevania
B) Metal Gear
C) Gradius
D) Contra

Q6. Sports Gaming

Which studio developed the FIFA video game series that dominated soccer gaming in the 90s and 2000s?

A) Konami
B) Sega
C) EA Sports
D) 2K Sports

Q7. Nintendo Rivalry

In the early 90s console wars, which game was bundled with the Sega Genesis to directly compete with Super Mario?

A) Ecco the Dolphin
B) Sonic the Hedgehog
C) Altered Beast
D) Streets of Rage

Q8. GTA City Match

Match each Grand Theft Auto city (A-D) with the real-world city it's based on (1-4):

GTA Cities:

A) Liberty City (GTA III)

B) Vice City

C) San Andreas (San Fierro)

D) Los Santos

Real Cities:

1. Los Angeles
2. New York City
3. Miami
4. San Francisco

Q9. Xbox Launch

Which game was the flagship launch title that helped sell the original Xbox in 2001?

A) Fable
B) Halo: Combat Evolved
C) Project Gotham Racing
D) Dead or Alive 3

Q10. Simulation City

Which game let you build cities, manage budgets, and watch tiny people complain about traffic, becoming one of the best-selling PC franchises of all time?

A) SimCity
B) Civilization
C) Age of Empires
D) Command & Conquer

Did You Know? Tear Down That Wall

Remember those grainy live shots from Berlin, anchors half shouting over crowds and car horns? The Cold War felt permanent, then a line at the Brandenburg Gate and a muddled press conference helped tip it over. On June 12, 1987, at the Brandenburg Gate, President Ronald Reagan declared, "Mr. Gorbachev, tear down this wall!" The phrase leapt past jamming, onto cassettes and radios, and into classrooms, a sound bite that outlived the podium.

Poland's trade union Solidarity was the first independent labor union in a Soviet-bloc country. Led by electrician Lech Wałęsa, it forced talks with the government and showed that organized, non-violent pressure could work. Wałęsa later became the first president of a democratic Poland in 1990, a signal that the region's politics were already shifting beneath the concrete.

The Night the Gate Opened

On the night of November 9, 1989, spokesman Günter Schabowski told reporters that East Germans could travel "sofort, unverzüglich," effectively immediately. The line came from a miscommunication. He had been handed a note about new travel rules but wasn't fully briefed and believed they took effect at once, not the following day. Within minutes, thousands moved toward Bornholmer Strasse. With no clear orders, officer Harald Jäger lifted the barrier around 11:30 p.m., and the flood began.

The Berlin Wall was a border system, not just a slab. It included an inner wall, a floodlit death strip, a patrol road, watchtowers, and the outer show wall. The death strip bristled with obstacles like anti-vehicle trenches, barbed wire, and tripwires that triggered flares and alarms while armed guards watched from towers. It ringed West Berlin for about 96 miles. More than 5,000 people escaped, and at least 140 died trying.

From Wall to Reunion

The opening set off what Germans called Die Wende, meaning "the Turning," a phrase for the great political changes of 1989–1990. It moved the country toward Wiedervereinigung, or reunification, on October 3, 1990. That meant joining two different currencies, two sets of laws, and two very different economies and social systems into one. Gorbachev kept Soviet tanks from rolling, and within a year the Soviet Union itself was gone.

Today Berlin displays its history in public. The East Side Gallery is the longest open-air gallery in the world, a 1,316-meter stretch painted with 100-plus murals, including Dmitri Vrubel's "My God, Help Me to Survive This Deadly Love," the famous Brezhnev-Honecker kiss. Memorials and museums mark the terror that stood here, while Potsdamer Platz's glass towers and lively neighbourhoods show how a once-divided city builds outward, together.

Historically, Berlin was carved into four Allied sectors after World War II, American, British, French in the west, and Soviet in the east, even though the rest of Germany was only split in two. That unusual arrangement left the city as a frontline of the Cold War, a fact still easy to miss if you only look at today's cafés and start-ups. Compare it to today's Demilitarized Zone in Korea, or the division of Vietnam during the war: Berlin was once a symbol of permanent division, but unlike those frozen borders, it eventually fused back together.

Modern Berlin is both a memorial and a magnet, where brass plaques and murals sit alongside buzzing tech hubs, sprawling street art, and a world-famous nightclub scene that keeps music going until sunrise. It's proof that a city once caged can now thrive on creativity, openness, and nonstop energy.

Round 17 Answers

No cheat codes here, time to see if your score is legendary or just "game over."

Q1. Answer: A) The ghosts turn blue and can be eaten

Power pellets flip the chase. The ghosts turn blue and flee, and Pac-Man can eat them for escalating points (200, 400, 800, 1600). The frightened timer gets shorter as levels rise, so late-game windows are tiny. Blinky, Pinky, Inky, and Clyde each have distinct AI personalities. Blinky chases you directly, Pinky tries to ambush ahead of you, Inky's behavior depends on both Blinky's position and yours, and Clyde just does whatever he feels like, often fleeing to the bottom-left corner. He's programmed to be unreliable, the least threatening ghost, which is why speedrunners call him "the coward."

Q2. Answer: True

Namco's US distributor Midway changed Puck Man to Pac-Man so bored teens with keys couldn't turn the P into an F on arcade cabinets. The name change was so urgent that Midway started mass-producing rebranded cabinets before Namco even gave permission. Vandalism prevention became instant branding. The original Japanese version kept Puck Man because katakana doesn't have that problem. The yellow circle with a missing slice was inspired by a pizza with one piece removed, according to creator Toru Iwatani.

Q3. Answer: A-4, B-5, C-1, D-2, E-3, F-6, G-7

Super Mario 64 launched the Nintendo 64 in 1996, proving 3D platformers could work with an analog stick. Composer Koji Kondo drew from Afro-Cuban rhythms and Latin jazz for Bob-Omb Battlefield's music, giving the game unexpected groove. GoldenEye and Ocarina of Time defined the N64's library. Sonic was Sega Genesis's mascot answer to Mario, deliberately colored electric blue to match Sega's logo and contrast Nintendo's red branding. Pac-Man ate quarters in arcades starting 1980. Halo became Xbox's killer app. Final Fantasy VII moved the JRPG crown to PlayStation in 1997 with three discs of FMV cutscenes that melted teenage brains.

Q4. Answer: B) They were an accidental timing bug players loved

Combos started as a happy accident. A timing quirk let one move cancel into another before the opponent recovered. Players discovered they could chain moves together, and it felt incredible. American players started calling them "combos" because the moves were literally combining due to animation canceling. Capcom noticed, loved it, leaned into it hard, and the entire fighting game genre was born. Now people lab combos for hours, count frame data, and argue about optimal punishes on Reddit. All because of a bug that should've been patched.

Q5. Answer: C) Gradius

The Konami Code debuted in Gradius on the NES in 1986. Developer Kazuhisa Hashimoto programmed it as a testing cheat because he was terrible at his own game and needed a way to beat it for playtesting. Up, Up, Down, Down, Left, Right, Left, Right, B, A became burned into gamer muscle memory. Contra popularized it the next year with the famous 30 lives bonus (because you needed them), which is why everyone associates it with that game. But the origin story belongs to a brutally hard space shooter, created by a developer who admitted he sucked.

Q6. Answer: C) EA Sports

EA Sports launched FIFA International Soccer in 1993 without real player names due to licensing costs. The highest-rated forward was "Andreas Blitzer," a completely made-up person. The game still dominated because EA secured FIFA's official license for tournaments and teams. They turned it into an annual release juggernaut that printed money for decades. Konami's Pro Evolution Soccer was technically superior for years, but FIFA had the licenses and the marketing budget. EA lost the FIFA license in 2023 and rebranded to EA Sports FC, proving even 30-year partnerships end when money gets weird.

Q7. Answer: B) Sonic the Hedgehog

Sega needed a mascot to challenge Nintendo's Mario dominance. Sonic launched in 1991 bundled with the Genesis, designed to show off speed with "blast processing" marketing hype. His electric blue color matched Sega's logo, ensuring every ad reinforced the brand war against Nintendo's red. Altered Beast was the original pack-in but couldn't compete with Mario. Sonic's attitude, speed, and "Genesis does what Nintendon't" ads turned the console war into an actual fight. By 1992, Sonic outsold Mario games. Then Sega fumbled the Saturn and Dreamcast so badly they quit hardware forever.

Q8. Answer: A-2, B-3, C-4, D-1

Liberty City is New York with the serial numbers filed off. Vice City went full 1980s Miami with neon, pastel suits, and Scarface vibes. San Fierro captured San Francisco's hills and cable cars, plus a huge forest called "The Big Smoke" modeled after redwood parks but containing literally nothing but trees to save development time. Los Santos is Los Angeles down to the street layout and Vinewood sign. Rockstar maps real cities with just enough changes to avoid lawsuits while keeping every landmark recognizable. GTA III dropped in October 2001 right after 9/11, so they cut content and dialed back certain missions to avoid being insensitive.

Q9. Answer: C) Project Gotham Racing

Project Gotham Racing launched with Xbox in November 2001 as a flagship title. The Kudos point system rewarded stylish driving, not just speed, inspired by developer Bizarre Creations' previous game Metropolis Street Racer on Dreamcast. You got points for drifting, drafting, and taking corners with flair. Halo was the other major launch title that actually sold the console. Fable came later in 2004. Dead or Alive 3 launched alongside but focused on the fighting game crowd. Without Halo's success, Project Gotham would've been remembered as the flagship that wasn't enough.

Q10. Answer: A) SimCity

Will Wright created SimCity in 1989 while trying to design traffic patterns for a helicopter combat game. He got so absorbed in building the city that he abandoned the combat game entirely. SimCity had no win condition, just endless urban planning problems. You zone residential, commercial, and industrial areas, build infrastructure, and watch citizens riot when you raise taxes. SimCity 2000 added underground layers and arcologies. The Sims spun off in 2000 as "people simulator" and became the best-selling PC game of all time. EA's disastrous SimCity 2013 launch with always-online DRM nearly killed the franchise until Cities: Skylines ate its lunch in 2015.

The Final Answer

So, you've made it to the end, still clutching your scorecard like it's the Declaration of Independence. Along the way, you wrestled with Mount Rushmore math, pieced together book releases from Lord of the Flies to Harry Potter, survived shark malfunctions and Woodstock hangovers, and even decoded presidential scandals with more flair than Congress. If your brain feels like it's just run a marathon across time zones, good. That's the point.

You've dined with emperors, sung with sitcom characters, argued over whether fries are really French, and maybe even learned why salt doesn't actually boil water faster. The fun of trivia isn't in getting every answer right. It's in remembering the stories that stick. Keep that curiosity sharp, keep quizzing friends mercilessly, and remember history, pop culture, food, and politics all share one thing. They're far stranger (and funnier) than fiction.

Printed in Dunstable, United Kingdom